THE
MEDICINE
BAG

THE MEDICINE BAG

SHAMANIC RITUALS & CEREMONIES FOR PERSONAL TRANSFORMATION

▲▽▲▽▲▽▲▽▲▽▲

DON JOSE RUIZ

Hierophantpublishing

Cover design by Emma Smith
Cover Art by Nicetoseeya | Shutterstock,
and photolinc | Shutterstock
Labyrinth illustration by Zoart Studio | Shutterstock
Medicine Wheel w/ Feathers illustration by
stevezmina1 | Getty Images
Other Illustrations by Garylarts

Hierophant Publishing
www.hierophantpublishing.com

Library of Congress Control Number: 2019952950
ISBN: 978-1-938289-87-3

Print book interior design by Frame25 Productions

DEDICATION

To all the women and men who have learned how to master and create healing in their lives, and who have left this sacred shamanic legacy to us from all the different shamanic traditions of the world.

To all those who are now healing their own minds, bodies, and spirits in order to better serve others as well as Mother Earth.

To the next generations of the keepers of the flame, who will carry on the sacred teachings of the medicine bag.

CONTENTS

FOREWORD

When my son Jose was eleven years old, I took him and his older brother Miguel Jr., who was fourteen at the time, to Madre Grande, a mountain in Southern California. While we'd visited the mountain previously for family events that included hiking and cookouts, Madre Grande also had special significance beyond that, as it is where my mother, Sarita, a *curandera,* or "faith healer," would often share with us the sacred teachings of our family's Toltec tradition. Sarita was the keeper of the wisdom tradition of our family for her generation.

After we arrived at Madre Grande that day, I asked the boys if they were ready to be initiated into the path of the Toltec, to which they both eagerly agreed. This coming-of-age ceremony took place approximately thirty years ago, and it marked the beginning of a long apprenticeship they would undertake to learn the ways of our ancestors, culminating years later in both becoming master teachers in their own right.

While Jose and Miguel Jr. share much in common, they have taken slightly different routes in sharing the teachings of our family in their own unique way. Miguel Jr. has brought the ideas to a largely mainstream community, while Jose has embraced the shamanic origin of the Toltec tradition, and explained these ancient teachings in a way the modern world can understand.

Unlike some forms of shamanism, the Toltec tradition places a special emphasis on unconditional love and personal healing as the means by which we create transformation in ourselves and the world. We teach that we are all the artists of our own lives, and that we have the power to change our lives if we don't like the ones we're living.

In fact, the truth is that *it's only when we change ourselves that we change the world*. This axiom has been stated in various ways by many of the great teachers in every spiritual tradition.

In my opinion, this message is needed today as much as ever. When we look around this beautiful planet, we see so many of our fellow humans suffering—mentally, emotionally, spiritually, and physically—and as a result they often feel blocked from the innate sense of self-love, joy, and peace that is available to us all.

It's time to heal from this kind of suffering, and the book you are holding in your hands right now can help you do exactly that. In the pages that follow, my son, don Jose Ruiz, will share specific rituals and ceremonies from our Toltec tradition that can help you come into harmony with your innermost self and the world around you.

The shamanic practices described here will teach you how to take the raw material of life—physical pieces of the natural world, along with your inner thoughts and intentions—and draw out their meaning and power through ceremony. This is the joining of spirit and substance, of intention and action, all with the purpose of helping yourself—and in turn, others on this beautiful planet.

To be our own healers, we must look into our wounds, not turn away from them, or try to ignore them. Doing so takes bravery and stamina, but it's only when we understand our wounds and heal them that we transform our lives.

In my opinion, there has never been a more important time to do this work. My hope is that you will take the tools Jose describes in these pages and create the life you deserve.

All my love,
Don Miguel Ruiz
Author of *The Four Agreements*

INTRODUCTION

In what is now south-central Mexico, between one thousand and three thousand years ago, the Toltec civilization was thriving. According to my family's oral tradition, the Toltec people were responsible for building the massive pyramid complex at Teotihuacán, about twenty-five miles northeast of modern-day Mexico City. The Toltec culture was revered by the Aztecs—who came after them and shared their Nahuatl tongue—for their accomplishments in art, writing, medicine, and religion.

But this characterization of the Toltec people tells only a small part of their great and fascinating legacy. Toltec society was in many ways centered on studying the human mind, with the goal of creating the best life possible. Beyond mere survival, or the pursuit of war-like domination over others, Toltec people were purposefully creative and expressive. In fact, the very name *Toltec* means "artist" in Nahuatl. The use of the word *artist* in this context expands beyond the meaning of a person who paints, sculpts, or makes traditional forms of art. The Toltecs taught that every one of us is an artist, and the art we are creating is the story of our lives. In a way, one could say that the Toltecs explored psychology and personal growth in profound ways thousands of years before the birth of Sigmund Freud or Carl Jung.

As mentioned, the Toltecs spoke the Nahuatl language, and I want to share a very important word in this language with you, because it will play a central role in the ideas presented in this book. That word is *Nagual*, and like many words in English, it has two meanings. First, *nagual* refers to the life force energy, or the divinity, that is inside you, me, and all things. Nagual energy is invisible, and yet nothing could exist or be alive without it. *Nagual* is also used to refer to the women and men who served as spiritual teachers, doctors, philosophers, and healers in the community. In this sense, *Nagual* means "one who is awake." Today, we call these men and women shamans. I am considered a Nagual in my Toltec tradition, but I also refer to myself as a shaman because it's the modern term used to describe the same calling.

Another thing I want to make clear is that because everyone has the nagual energy inside them, everyone has the potential to be a Nagual, or shaman. In one sense, you already are. Simply possessing the gift of being alive in human form means that you have a choice in how you want to live your life. This makes you an artist, a creator of your life. Many people, however, are creating unconsciously—as if they were painting in their sleep.

It's more important than ever that we remember and value this inherent energy that we all possess—because we can use it to fashion a better way of being in the world. In this book, I share a wealth of rituals, practices, and ceremonies that are designed to tap into this conscious, creative energy, to help you awaken to your creative abilities and fulfill your potential. Through the repetitive practice of ritual, we are able to wake up.

The Power of Ritual and Ceremony

In the broadest sense, virtually every human on this beautiful planet participates in a host of daily rituals. We brush our teeth, wash our bodies, feed ourselves, go to work, and perhaps tend to the needs of children and elders. We may have other rituals we perform primarily for fun, such as enjoying a regular date night with our spouse, taking an annual summer vacation, or planning a family reunion. Going a bit deeper, many of us have also developed religious or spiritual practices that take the form of ritual. These might include ceremonies on certain days of the year, or on special occasions such as births, deaths, or marital unions.

While most of us participate in these kinds of rituals and ceremonies already, the rituals in this book are geared toward a wholly different space. They seek to aid your journey of *awakening*. What do I mean by awakening? I use the word *awakening* here because in my family's Toltec tradition we say that humans are dreaming all the time. Let me explain.

First, each person is always in the midst of what we call the *Personal Dream,* which is your own perspective—how you see the world around you and how you make sense of it through the stories you tell yourself about what you perceive. Second, there is what we call the *Dream of the Planet,* or the sum of all our Personal Dreams. Together they form the basis for how we create the world around us and communicate with one another.

So I don't say that the rituals and ceremonies here can help us awaken from the dream, but rather that they help us awaken *to the fact that we are dreaming.* To dream and to tell stories are what the mind does. You cannot stop dreaming; you can only become aware of yourself as a dreaming animal and work with this double-edged gift to change the dream itself. Therefore, the primary aim of the practices in this book is to help you wake up to the knowledge that you are dreaming and create your life in the form of a beautiful dream.

If we look around, it's easy to see that so many of our fellow humans are living in a type of nightmare, where their actions come from a place of fear rather than unconditional love. Living this way, they cause harm to themselves and others, from something relatively small like an unkind remark all the way up to and including wars between countries.

Toltec shamanism aims to bring love to every part of your dream—especially to the areas of your own dream where you find yourself suffering. After all, love is the power that transforms a bad dream into a beautiful one.

Rituals and ceremonies, when they are done consciously, with the right intent, can go beyond the realm of mere thought and make manifest your positive desires in the physical world. In this way, rituals and ceremonies serve to further your personal transformation, wherever you currently stand on your journey.

I would also like to mention that the word *intent* has a special meaning in the Toltec tradition. When you bring intent to something in this context, it means you bring your focus, calm and clear, to a specific thing—whether it's an object, a wish, a situation, or even another person. Your intent is powerful, and learning how to direct it consciously is one of the things you will gain from this book.

When you undertake a ritual or ceremony in this way, you are also tapping into the powerful nagual energy around you, calling forth this energy to help you on the path.

Coming into Balance

As you have undoubtedly noticed, there appears to be a great schism in the current Dream of the Planet. On one hand, we live in a time that boasts the greatest freedom and prosperity the world has ever known, and on the other, many in our human family are in constant conflict with one another, others are heavily medicated or self-medicating, and many have forgotten the importance of respecting the precious resources of Mother Earth. Nature herself is suffering at our hands, and the survival of our species and the beautiful world we inhabit are ultimately at stake.

What will come next? How can we move from chaos and imbalance to a healing place of alignment? Our first step is to change ourselves, and the practices in this book are designed to help you do exactly that.

I would like to share with you a story that encapsulates the power of ritual:

For millennia, Wolf was the steward of a wide valley with forest and field, river and stream. One day, a hooded figure wearing a long, gray cloak arrived in the valley. The figure watched in horror and fear as Wolf killed an elk. In return, the figure murdered the wolf and all his children. In Wolf's absence, as time passed, the valley fell into disarray. The river became chaotic, flooding its banks one season and drying up completely in another. Songbirds flew away into the sky, followed by crows and eagles. The beaver went missing. Trees and grass were stripped bare under the relentless grazing of elk and deer. Each lonely night passed by silent and empty without the howls of the pack.

The figure in gray watched all of this, perplexed, until one morning a ray of dawn sunlight hit his face. With the light came a whispering voice that brought the message that it was time for Wolf to return.

The figure made an offering to invite Wolf back. As soon as Wolf came home to the valley, he began to do his sacred tasks: Howl. Chase. Connect. Move. Kill. Give.

These were the rituals of the wolf. These were the ways the sacred steward-ship of the valley took form.

Wolf moved the elk and deer through the valley by howl and chase. The graz-ers flourished and moved through the land, leaving tree and grass and brush to seek the sun and grow tall. The raven fol-lowed the wolf pack to every corner of the valley, sharing its gifts of carrion with the eagles and bears. The beaver emerged again, caretaker of the river, felling trees and stacking them into dams that formed deep, cold pools for fish and frogs.

The cloaked figure reveled in the change as the river returned steadily to its bed. The ritual of renewal was complete, and the fear that led the figure to kill the wolf was gone. In its place was gratitude for all things as they are, and all things playing their part.

This modern parable is remarkable because it is true. Eighty years ago, humans (wearing a cloak of fear and greed) decimated the wolf population in Yellowstone National Park. Then, in 1995, a small number of wolves were returned to the park. They seeded new life in extraordinary ways, restoring the ecosystem, repairing the broken food web, and even stabilizing the physical structure of the river.

Like the lesson in this story, rituals and ceremonies teach us to act from a place of love instead of fear, as this is the way to come into balance.

The Mind's Addiction to Suffering

As I mentioned, *nagual* describes the energy force in the universe that gives life to all things. The nagual energy is never-ending, always present, and filled with peace and well-being. And yet, at the same time, my family's tradition recognizes that the human mind is addicted to suffering. It's this addiction that causes so much of our misery and prevents us from seeing the beauty that surrounds us.

When I tell people that one of the greatest problems facing humanity is the mind's addiction to suffering, they sometimes look at me in confusion or disbelief, so please allow me to explain further.

Consider all the ways we cause suffering in our own lives. We work and struggle to acquire things we don't need, and then get angry or sad if we don't get them. When others don't behave as we think they should, we might judge and withhold our love as a form of punishment (this can happen in both big and little ways). And, of course, we inflict suffering on others and ourselves through physical violence and war.

Still, this list does not include the most prevalent way we cause suffering to ourselves, and that is the suffering we generate through our own thinking. We are the only animal on this planet to reject ourselves. We tell ourselves that we're not good enough, that we're not worthy of love, and we replay stories of regret from our past or fears of what might happen in the future.

The mind spins these judgments, fears, and regrets at a moment's notice, often when something triggers a memory or a deep-seated anxiety. By continuing a chatter of negative storytelling—comparing, judging, and looking for problems—the mind creates most of the suffering that we experience.

Every moment has the potential to be beautiful, yet the mind is so addicted to suffering that it will create misery instead, often out of thin air, summoning and maintaining a kind of inner chaos that can drain our energy and disconnect us from the life force that surrounds and supports us.

I also want to make clear that this isn't a personal failure, as virtually all humans have this addiction to suffering to some degree or another. As you notice this tendency inside yourself, please don't use it as ammunition to beat yourself up further, but rather acknowledge it as a habit of the mind. The first step to ending any addiction is to notice that it exists, and to realize that you are the only one who can change it. The journey out of this suffering is one of awakening, and for many generations my family has taught this path. We have been teachers, guides, and friends of humanity—all the way down to and including my grand-mother Sarita and my father, don Miguel Ruiz.

However, we have always done this know-ing (as all shamans do) that each person must find his or her own way on the journey. After all, we are each creating our own individual dream. The mind is built to dream—we can't stop this dreaming, but once we awaken to this truth, we can begin to notice the ways we lace our dreams with negativity. The rituals and cer-emonies in this book can help reorient the sto-rytelling mind toward love and away from fear.

On this journey, what if I told you that you could carry with you a very powerful, ancient tool around your neck and held close to your heart? The medicine bag is such a tool, both literally and metaphorically.

In a literal sense, a medicine bag is usually a small pouch, about the size of your hand, which is often worn around the neck and can also be carried in your pocket or handbag. It can vary in size, material, and contents; the idea to remember is that a bag like this has been used by thousands of people before you as they progressed on their own journeys of awakening. It may carry written prayers, sticks, bones, rocks, feathers, or seashells. It may contain an object that is the symbol of a vision, a piece of nature from a meaningful place, a talisman of an animal totem. The contents of the medicine bag are physical representations that guide the inner journey of the wearer. In the next chapter, I'll go into detail about how to make or choose your own medicine bag, and the remaining chapters in this book will explain how to begin creating or choosing items to carry inside to help you on your own journey.

In a metaphorical sense, we each have an inner medicine bag that we've been carrying with us for most of our lives. If we don't realize this, then it has also probably never occurred to us to wonder what tools we've been carrying around in it. I'm talking about the tools we reach for out of habit: judgments, angry reactions, regrets, fears, and more. We put these tools to work building negative realities for ourselves and others in a constant effort to feed the mind's addiction to suffering.

Part of our journey together in this book will be about removing the negative practices and beliefs from your internal medicine bag and replacing them with things like self-confidence, faith, peace, courage, access to your intuition, and most critically, love for yourself and others. Love is the most important tool of all in your inner medicine bag; in fact, it is the birthplace of every other positive tool you can ever possess.

The contents of your outer medicine bag have a mysterious ability to support the transformation of your inner medicine bag. Meaningful objects, prayers, and symbols of the natural world help you call on the strength of the nagual that is inside and all around you. Furthermore, the rituals and ceremonies in these pages are designed to open pathways into powerful concepts and abilities like discovering your own divinity, intuition, healing, and awareness. Through these rituals, even as the mind continues its powerfully convincing dream, you can recognize the truth: that everything is already perfect—as it should be—and this includes you.

How to Use This Book

This is not a book of philosophy. Yes, there will be explanations to set the stage, but this is really a book of practices that you can do to help you along your path.

For this reason, imagine you are holding a kind of cookbook, filled with inspiration, techniques, and recipes. As with a cookbook, you will want to try the rituals in this book, recreate them, adapt them, and most importantly put them into practice in your own life. Some will appeal to you more than others, and that's okay. You should only undertake what feels right for you, and even then, you can adapt them in whatever way you feel is necessary for your own personal path.

The path of the shaman—the Nagual—is an individual journey. Rituals, likewise, must be one-of-a-kind, adaptable to your own individual circumstances. The rituals in this book are meant to be practiced with creative intention by each shaman, for a shaman follows his or her own deep inner truth—not the authority or tradition of others for their own sake.

You may choose to read this book in order by chapter, or you may choose to go directly to the chapter that calls you. I would recommend reading chapter one in all cases, because here we will cover the importance of healing, as well as how to create two important tools that we will refer to throughout the book: the medicine bag and the personal altar.

I would also like to say a few words about getting ready for a ritual or ceremony. As you prepare and gather the items you need for the practices in this book, I encourage you to do so with sacred intention. This isn't merely "setup time"; this too is part of your ceremony. In some ways, this time of preparation can be just as powerful, if not more so, than the ceremony itself.

For instance, I have a friend who once attended a changing of the seasons ritual at another friend's home. When she arrived, she and her friend spent well over an hour setting up the altar and making little changes to it, bringing flowers in from the garden, telling each other stories of past celebrations, listening to music, and dancing a bit as they arranged and rearranged items on the table. When they were finished, the altar radiated with love and celebration . . . and nothing more seemed necessary. The preparation had become the ceremony itself.

So as you prepare and gather the items you'll need for a particular ceremony, rather than rushing through this time, slow down and bring awareness to your movements. Let your heart and mind be in the present moment during this process, as doing so signals to your inner self that this is a special time you are setting aside in your day.

Lastly, I would like to point out that as the very name suggests, a medicine bag is primarily about healing, and the truth is that when we heal ourselves, we transform ourselves in the process. When we are seeking personal transformation, most often it is because we are suffering. Our addiction to suffering is a kind of illness, and when we take the medicine we need to heal, the result is transformation. The medicine is always love, and every time we choose it, the healing cycle happens over and over again, bringing us into alignment with the nagual energy inside us.

1

THE IMPORTANCE OF HEALING

In the Toltec tradition, we recognize that every human is an artist (remember the word *Toltec* means artist), and the art we create is the story of our lives. As my father don Miguel Ruiz likes to say, "If you don't like the story you're living in, you are the only one who can change it."

Healing ourselves is what makes lasting change possible. The medicine bag is designed to help you do exactly this.

I was taught the importance of healing from one of the most powerful shamans I have ever known: my grandmother. She was the keeper of the oral tradition of our family, and she shared her wisdom with my father, my brothers, and the rest of her family so that it might be carried down, enhanced, and put into practice for generations to come. This is her great, ongoing gift.

My grandmother was an extremely powerful *curandera* (faith healer), whose own self-healing practice connected her to the strength of generations that came before her, to nature, to her deep religious faith, and to the healing power of Mother Earth.

Through my grandmother's example, I learned three key things:

1. When we heal ourselves, we build a strong foundation for our lives.

2. When we heal ourselves, we are preparing humanity—not just our loved ones, whom we touch directly, but really all people—to heal themselves as well.

3. When we heal ourselves, we claim our place as Toltec warriors.

For those of you who are unfamiliar with the Toltec warrior, this doesn't refer to physical violence, but rather to those who have made a commitment to watching their own minds and rooting out any negativity they find there. The Toltec warrior is one who makes a commitment to end the mind's addiction to suffering.

When I reference the Toltecs in this capacity, I don't mean the ancient civilization that thrived twenty-five hundred years ago. I am talking about the Toltecs alive now, those of us who realize that we are the artists of our lives and who have committed to creating a beautiful masterpiece. At the same time, it's important to remember that we're not at the beginning of this work. We build on the understanding of past generations, who have passed down this knowledge and helped bring us to this point. Now we get to make the choice to transcend, grow, and blossom. I say this to remind you that while a self-healing practice can only come from you and your own intent, you are not without support. As you work through your own healing, remember that you are held up by the strength and love of the warriors who have come before you.

To begin your ceremonial journey, you will create two specials tools—ones that we'll refer to time and time again throughout the rest of this book: the medicine bag and the personal altar.

Your Medicine Bag

A medicine bag is a traditional object in many indigenous cultures that holds a variety of sacred items unique to its owner. It is a physical touchstone that keeps you centered on your path as you move through the living world. In times of stress, it can act as a ballast to hold you steady on what is most important, and its weight and texture act as a constant reminder that you are a part of a greater story, walking a path of healing and personal growth.

Some people carry small medicine bags with them on a thong or cord around their necks or in a purse or pocket, and others may have slightly larger bags that they take with them to ceremonies. Many traditional medicine bags are made by hand from animal hides or leather. While tradition is important, any established pattern must grow and change along with the culture in order for it to retain its power and relevance. You may find that you prefer to purchase a premade medicine bag, or that you gravitate toward a medicine bag made of cotton, linen, or felt. The bag itself should feel right to you, whether traditional or nontraditional, because what is most important is the inner work you will do with it. You will draw from your deepest self to fill your bag with healing energy and items with profound significance.

If you choose to create your own medicine bag, you must first decide on its size. A small personal bag you carry around your neck or tucked in a pocket or purse might typically fit in the palm of your hand. A simple drawstring bag is relatively easy to make by cutting two pieces of fabric (or leather if you are comfortable with the techniques of leatherworking), sewing them together on three sides, turning them inside out, and then sewing a string or cord into the top for the drawstring. A larger bag for ceremonial items can be made in much the same way, at whatever scale you like. There are a number of tutorials online that can help with this.

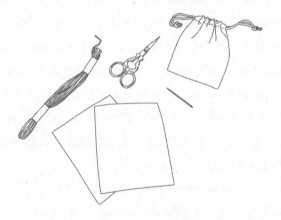

Once you've made your bag, you may wish to decorate it with beads, embroidery, or painted symbols unique to your path and that have special meaning for you. The bag itself is a sacred object in its own right; spend the same amount of attention and time on its construction or selection as you would the objects inside it.

If you choose to purchase a premade bag, look at several different options and wait for the right bag to call to you—you will know it when you see it. Hold different options in your hand if you can, and see if any of them "feel right," or if you perceive any natural signs at the time. Did birds fly overhead when you picked up a certain bag? Did you catch a familiar scent in the air? There's no need to rush this process. Often when we allow a sacred object to choose us, instead of the other way around, we end up with something perfect for us in ways we wouldn't have consciously chosen.

Once you have found or created your medicine bag, what you put in it is entirely up to you. Take your time with this. Resist the urge to add everything all at once. Instead, take the opportunity to spend time in meditation to discern what belongs in your medicine bag, and what may be best to leave on your altar at home (which we will look at next). These items may include small stones, gifts from your spirit animal (feathers, bits of fur), dried plants, tiny seashells, prayers written on paper. Think of your most precious personal items that together represent your unique spirit and embody a powerful symbol of your journey. In the chapters that follow, I will be making suggestions on creating items that you can include in your medicine bag—ones that can help you heal and transform.

When your medicine bag is complete, you may want to set aside some time to bless your bag by letting it soak in the rays of the sun or the moon, or praying/chanting over it as you focus on its new role as a touchstone for you on your spiritual or healing path.

Finally, allow your medicine bag to evolve as you do. You may feel directed to add or subtract items based on dreams, sacred walks, vision journeys, healing needs, or encounters with your spirit animal. Let your intuition guide you in this—there is no right or wrong way. The bag is a sacred blessing that goes with you wherever you go.

Your Personal Altar

In addition to the power of the medicine bag, many traditional cultures recognize the importance of creating a sacred place for spiritual reflection, one that unites the seen and unseen worlds. A personal altar is a reflection of this ancient concept—an honored place, set aside and tended mindfully, imbued with beauty and devotion, where the sacred and the everyday meet. In some ways, your medicine bag already functions like a small portable altar, as it contains items of deeply sacred power that resonate with your personal path. Likewise, creating your home altar fosters your unique journey, expands the power of your sacred purpose into your whole home, and offers a beloved space for ceremonial practice.

In the Toltec tradition, your personal altar serves as a metaphor for your unique spirit and your place in the universe. There are no rules for altar creation; your altar may be minimalist and simple, or bursting with color and texture. At your altar, you can say prayers or mantras, set and reflect on your intent, meditate, perform rituals and ceremonies, make offerings, and sing songs. Like a medicine bag, it is a physical reminder of the journey you are on, a home base for your divine heart.

You may want to change the seasonal theme of your altar, and you can honor your loved ones who have passed on before you by placing their pictures there (both of these practices will be covered later in this book). An altar is a place of rest from the hectic pace of everyday life, where you can notice if the mind is caught in a trap of suffering. An altar is a signal to the spirits and powers of the living world that you are ready to move forward on your path.

Each person's altar will be one-of-a-kind, but here are some suggestions to get you started:

First, find a place in your home to dedicate to this work—the top of a dresser or cupboard, a small end table, a bookcase, a nightstand, a fireplace mantle, an outside garden nook. You might even consider making your altar on a plank of wood or a small table or cart with wheels so you can stash it away when not in use. Altars can be adapted to any surface or size—so don't worry if all you can manage in the beginning is one corner of your dresser. Even a simple votive candle with one or two small items can hold the space and focus your intent as powerfully as the most elaborate altar.

Once you've chosen your spot you may want to clear and consecrate the space, making sure it's free of dust and cleansing it energetically with incense or a salt ceremony (see chapter nine). Once the space is ready, take some time to choose your altar objects. You may already have items around your home that you know will have a place on your altar, or you may need to spend some time in nature or seeking out objects that have meaning for you. You might want to include fresh flowers; crystals; natural items from sacred walks, such as pine cones, seashells, feathers, or stones; glass bottles filled with water from a special river, lake, or spring; bells; prayer books or other sacred texts; cups or bowls to hold water, herbs, earth, stones, or small objects; pictures of loved ones; statues or pictures of spirits or deities; candles or incense burners . . . the possibilities are truly endless.

When you have your altar arranged, set aside some time to light the candles, burn some incense, play some music. Pick up each object, considering its meaning and personal significance, and say a small prayer. Once your altar is established, you can return to it anytime, even for a few moments, to refresh your sense of purpose and connect with the living world. Don't feel obligated to perform long, elaborate ceremonies—even the simple act of picking up an altar item and holding it in your hands and asking for a blessing can reinvigorate your day.

Your altar is also your art. In your altar you will find an organic, spiritual reflection of the story of your life. Let its beauty be a reminder of how beautiful you are, as well as a window through which you can reach out to the unseen worlds.

A Commitment to Healing Yourself

Once you have established these two important tools in whatever way works for you, it's time to take your first ritual step toward personal healing. This ceremony is based on one that I learned from my grandmother. It serves as an initiation and commitment to self-healing and produces a powerful reminder object that will assist in your ongoing healing journey. In this practice, you will combine the items with your picture to align their beauty and potency with yourself. Performing this ceremony symbolizes your realization that you are the artist of your life and you recognize that healing yourself is the first step to creating the masterpiece that is your life story.

Prepare and gather:

- A photo of yourself

- A glass jar or other small container with a lid

- A few small, disposable objects that represent healing for you or are personally meaningful and attractive (e.g., seashells, flowers, stones, driftwood, pine cones, bits of colorful fabric)

- Incense (optional)

- Water

To begin, put your photo and disposable objects inside the container. If you are using incense, crumble a tiny bit of that up and add it to your container too. Then fill the container with water. Water is a universal symbol for life and, like air, a conduit for energy exchange between objects. We are all connected through the air we breathe and the water we exchange through our bodies.

Next, set your intent on healing and becoming the artist of your life, staying open to the breath and any sensations that come up for you, and say the following mantra out loud:

I commit to ongoing healing of my deepest self, to opening my heart, to caring for my body, to caring for my mind, to ending the addiction to suffering. I am the artist of my life, and I am ready to create my masterpiece.

Then, put the lid on the jar and set it somewhere undisturbed for three days. You have now created a powerful gestation container, one where the energy of the objects can be unified with your own energy. Over the next three days, each time you see or remember the jar, take a moment to feel the power of your intent and send that positive energy into it.

After three days, drain the water from the jar and remove your photo.

This picture now holds the power of the objects, the water, and your intention. While it is still wet, hold the picture between your palms and close your eyes. Feel grateful for the energy within it. After that, let your picture dry in the sun to absorb more powerful energy, and then put it in a meaningful place—perhaps in your medicine bag, on your altar, or between the pages of a journal or book that you read regularly. The important thing is that you put it in a special place where you will see it often, because it will remind you of your commitment to being a healer of yourself and the artist of your life.

I love this ceremony because it sets your intent to heal yourself and provides you with a physical representation of that intent. Both of these are expressed in the photo you have imbued with the energy of these objects. The photo now has this energy—and so do you.

2

ALIGNING WITH THE POWER OF NATURE

Every spring my father, my brother Miguel Jr., and I travel to Sedona, Arizona, for an annual event called the Gathering of the Shamans. Just a short distance from the Grand Canyon, the area that is now called northern Arizona is sacred to many Native American tribes, including the Hopi, Yavapai, Havasupai, and Navajo.

If you ever visit, it's easy to see why. The red rocks of Sedona are a unique combination of beauty and power. Home to many vortexes (energy centers), Sedona has long been a destination for seekers to help accelerate inner exploration, meditation, and healing. The more well-known Grand Canyon stretches on for over 220 miles, having been carved into its breathtaking and dramatic shape by the movement of the Colorado River over the course of millions of years. The canyon leaves thousands of visitors each year speechless with awe in the face of the sweeping dance of earth and sky and the immeasurable power of water to wear down seemingly immovable stone. Its sheer immensity is at once humbling and inspiring.

While seeing the magnificence of Sedona or the Grand Canyon can stop the thinking mind in its tracks, you don't need to travel to northern Arizona to experience the beauty and benefits of communing with nature. Nature is all around us—it is the literal air we breathe and water we drink, and we are in no way separate from it. We *are* nature, and nature is us. To be human is to be a part of all life—complex, evolving, interconnected. To live in a way that reflects the truth that all life is fundamentally connected is to walk the path of the shaman.

Because it is life, the natural world is replete with power that both creates and destroys. Water may arrive in the form of life-giving rain or terrifying floods. Fire may cook our food and keep us warm through winter, or it may decimate entire forests. A cooling breeze may be welcome on a hot summer day, but tornadoes and hurricanes wreak unimaginable damage every year. And earthquakes shake our strongest buildings, even as we depend on the stable earth beneath our feet every single day. For these reasons and more, nature deserves our gratitude and our respect.

Nature is also a great healer. Even modern science is catching up to this ancient wisdom in measurable ways. The *New York Times* reported in 2018 that a variety of studies have suggested that exposure to trees and plants may strengthen the human immune system and also lower stress hormones and blood pressure.

This would be no surprise to the shamans of my family's tradition, especially my grandmother, who taught us a powerful ceremony to tap into the energy of trees that she often used in her healing work.

She would point out that fallen branches and leaves, which are often considered "trash" in the modern world, are important symbols of the power of nature. They have grown through the power of Mother Earth and Father Sun; they have been caressed by wind and drunk deeply of the water. The thinking mind very often takes for granted nature's unmatched ability to create. Even the most incredible structures or fascinating technology built by humans can never compete in complexity with a single leaf. For this reason, I would like to begin this chapter on nature with a ceremony based on what she taught us.

Communing with Nature

Prepare and gather:

- A jar, bottle, or thermos filled with water

- A small garden trowel for digging (optional)

To begin, find a quiet place in nature where you can be alone and undisturbed for at least thirty minutes. While the more remote the better, this can be done in your backyard as well. Collect two or three small branches that have fallen from the trees nearby, ones that have some leaves still on them.

Once you have gathered a few branches with leaves, place them in a small pile in front of you. Take a few moments to reflect on how these branches came to be and what they represent: it all started with a seed, which took root in Mother Earth, was christened by life-giving water, touched by the warmth and light of Father Sun, nurtured by the air, and grew up, extending toward the sky. Think of how important the leaves are in the process; they take in the water, photosynthesize energy from the sun, and pull in carbon dioxide from the air. Now they have fallen to the earth, where they will decompose and fertilize the soil for new growth to occur. These branches are miracles, representative of the power of life and Mother Nature. These branches are symbols of life and its cycles.

Next, open your container of water and pour a small amount over the branches, including the leaves. Let the water soak in for a few moments, and then say the following mantra:

> Let these branches embody this truth:
>
> that all things in nature make
> their way in cycles,
>
> transforming from one thing into the next,
> forever and ever, for always and right now.
>
> I thank them for their gifts, for sharing
> their energy and power,
>
> and I return them to the earth
> they came from.

Next, remove some of the leaves and gently rub them up and down a small portion of your arms, inviting the power of nature into your heart. You are now communing with the branches, a symbol for all life, and welcoming their energy into you.

When you have finished rubbing the leaves on your arms, sit quietly for as long as you'd like, absorbing the sights, sounds, and smells of nature as you do so. This is your true home, the cradle for all life.

To close the ceremony, scoop some soil from the ground with your trowel and partially cover the pile of branches with it. In this way you are symbolically returning the branches to the ground. They don't need to be fully buried, as nature will determine their best course. As you do so, offer a prayer of thanks and gratitude to these branches and to all the elements of the natural world for making them possible.

You may choose to place a leaf in your medicine bag, and when you are in a big city or a place that seems far removed from the splendor of nature, it will be your connection. Or set it on your altar as a reminder of the awesome power of nature. One day this leaf will dry and crumble, and then you will know it is time to do this ceremony again.

Aligning with Cycles

Nature is also about cycles. Day turns to night. Seasons change as the Earth moves around the sun. A seed sprouts to become a plant, and then later that plant dies and fertilizes the soil where a new seed will grow. Even though cycles are all around us, the Western mind persists in finding linear patterns in almost everything, though science is now recognizing some of the flaws in this type of thinking.

I witnessed a good example of this change in the Western approach to nature one day when a friend's son came home from school with a science project. He was studying what they call the "food web." Now, when I went to school, and perhaps you too, it was called the "food chain."

This change in terminology is key.

The food chain model is very linear, and it suggested that one thing ate another all the way up to the apex of a pyramid—which is where human beings and other predators sat, fat and happy. My mind could never quite grasp all the inconsistencies this created. What about the plants and creatures that nobody really ate, like poison oak or skunks or puffer fish? Were they also at the top of a pyramid? More importantly, was eating and being eaten the whole point of the cycle of life? Weren't there other ways that each animal's life cycle enriched and challenged the others? This was certainly the case in the story of the wolves returning to Yellowstone. Even if we can't always see a direct relationship, the balance of the whole valley depends on the strength of each part. For this reason, the idea of a food web feels both more accurate and more exciting than a food chain.

As we look around at the Dream of the Planet, it's easy to see that the linear thinking that made up the old food chain model is still the predominant construction for many things, including the "progression" of our lives, or history itself. We are often encouraged to go to school, go to work, get a relationship, have children—whatever we do, we had better move on to the "next thing" in life, with each milestone promising happiness. But does this type of linear progression ever produce lasting happiness?

The Toltec tradition invites you to move past the view of life as a linear trip that goes from A to B to C and see it in terms of cycles instead. This simple shift in mind-set can help bring you into harmony with nature, which always moves in cycles, and with life itself. Think of how energy moves, how water and other elements change from liquid to solid to gas, how plants and animals grow and propagate. Cycles reflect how we sleep and wake, our natural seasons, the spin and arc of the Earth in space, the flow of generations, and so much more. In shamanic terms, when we stop thinking of life in straight lines and embrace cycles, we see that there are seasons for everything—our relationships, our health, our finances and careers. We can save ourselves a ton of time and energy by not planting crops in the winter, literally and metaphorically.

On closer inspection, we find that this straight line thinking only occurs in the human mind. Since our perspective comes from inside the mind, it can be tough to accept the idea that linear thinking is a human invention. But remember that the human mind once thought the Earth was flat and now we know it is a sphere. We also now know for a fact that energy cannot be created or destroyed, only changed into something new. The truth is that nothing begins or ends, really.

As we discover the benefits of moving past linear thinking, we see the wisdom of natural cycles can help us in many moments of life.

When we are having trouble with some aspect of our lives, for example, we can remember that all things in nature experience some kind of death and rebirth, and usually some kind of rest or hibernation. This can bring us hope. The darkest days of winter will turn the corner at the solstice, making way for just a bit more sunlight with each passing day. Spring will come again. Going further, being in tune with the seasons can foster a beautiful and essential acceptance of things as they are, an ever-present reminder of the teaching "this too shall pass." There is no better master than nature to help us learn this lesson. The sky is constant, and the clouds will pass. The bud of today will be a bloom tomorrow and then a fruit.

In addition, passing cycles and seasons offer a multitude of opportunities to celebrate, as well as to slow down and savor, this one precious life we are creating. This is true of a summer solstice bonfire or a festival of lights in the depth of winter with candles and singing. Seasons can remind us to slow down and reconnect, and they can also spur us to vigorous action— spring cleaning, for example, or doubling down on work at harvest time in the fall.

The seasons of our lifetime are no different. It is so gratifying to be in tune with and celebrate the cycles of growth and maturity from a child being born to coming into adulthood and having their own children—even a mindful death is a great gift.

One caveat here: we may also find that we have certain ideas about the seasons of our lives that aren't true, and when we become aware of them, we can change the agreements with ourselves. For instance, I have a dear friend who was devoted to her career for decades. She loved it, thrived, and brought great good to the world through her efforts. She decided to retire, but when she did, she found almost immediately that her beliefs about this season of her life needed updating. From her parents (who had disliked their jobs in a way she never did) and from society at large, she got the idea that she had to be "done" being productive at the age of sixty-five. But this was precisely the moment she was most experienced and wise. My friend was able to work with her feelings around this seasonal change in her life and ended up with a deeper commitment to continuing the work she loves to do and at which she excels.

When we look deeply at life we see that cycles are everywhere, and one of the most powerful ways to remind ourselves of this is to create a seasonal altar, adding to it and taking things away with each change of season.

Though they look different depending on where you live, the seasons shape our world. They fill our senses with color, light, smell, and temperature and keep a steady rhythm throughout our lives. Each season has its own special significance, and when you embrace the artistry of your life, you can paint your reality with even more depth and richness by aligning with the seasons—and doing so can help you remember to align with life rather than to fight against it.

The Seasonal Altar

Prepare and gather:

- Seasonal gifts from nature: pine cones, flowers, animal bones, seeds, leaves, rocks

- Photos of people and places that evoke the seasons of the year or stages of life

- Written memories of the natural world and time spent there

- Poems and prayers in praise of nature's cycles (anything from Walt Whitman to native oral histories)

- Incense or candles

If you've already established your personal home altar as outlined in chapter one you may choose to decorate this altar with seasonal items, or you may want to create an entirely different seasonal altar to mark the cycle of the year. A separate seasonal altar is a great opportunity to build a temporary outdoor altar of only natural items that may biodegrade or scatter over the course of time, which teaches the fundamental truth that in an organic world, change is constant.

Here are some guidelines regarding a few of the themes that each season often embodies. Bear in mind that depending on where you live, your experience of winter or summer may be very different from the descriptions below. Don't hesitate to adapt your seasonal altar to fit your region or intuition.

Winter

Winter is traditionally a fallow time, in which the plants and animals in temperate climates go to sleep. Likewise, we often turn inward and rediscover the power of stillness, comfort, and time spent with friends and family. Winter is also a time to recognize that hardship is a normal part of life and that darkness is always followed by light.

Winter altars may include candles or other sources of light and mirrors or other reflective surfaces to amplify it, plus winter fruits, such as pomegranates and citrus, and evergreen branches.

Spring

The season of reawakening, birth, and resurrection, we celebrate the rites of spring with colorful symbols of fertility and renewal. This is a wonderful time to plant seeds—not only in the soil but also in our lives—and to start new projects, preparing the way for growth and opportunity and savoring both the warmth and the mud that the season brings.

Your spring altar and ceremonies may include eggs, seeds, and branches with buds and flowers, such as yellow forsythia or pink cherry blossoms. This is also a wonderful time to do some spring cleaning and throw open your windows to fresh air physically and symbolically.

Summer

In summer, our gardens come into fullness, spilling over with juicy berries and earthy tomatoes. This is a time to enjoy, to soak in the fullness that life has to offer. Traditional summer activities draw us to the water's edge at lakes and the sea or high into the mountains where we can enjoy clear, refreshing air. Psychically, this can translate into a reconnection with the power of the sun, which gives us life and warmth, and with water, which brings the dual qualities of strength and fluidity.

Summer altars may include items from summer travels, garden fruits and vegetables, and meaningful objects found while hiking or beachcombing. Colorful fabrics might be a welcome addition. At this time of year, as well as in the "summer" of your lifetime, you can bring in an appreciation for the fullness of all you have accomplished. Enjoy the fruits of your labor and share the bounty with others.

Autumn

As the days get shorter, plants and animals begin the joyous work of preparing for winter, and we celebrate festivals of abundance and harvest. Squash, apples, and pears ripen into their fullness, and that very ripeness lives just on the edge of inevitable decay and death. Trees change color and shed their leaves.

This is a time of year to make sure your affairs are in order, to take stock of how far you have progressed toward your goals, and to prepare for difficulties ahead. Fall festivals throughout the world often hold within them a celebration of death—notably Halloween and Dia de los Muertos. This is a time of remembrance and calling on the wisdom of ancestors, as well as an opportunity to get more comfortable with this part of the cycle.

Your fall altar may include pine cones, squash, and colorful leaves. It may be an altar of remembrance for loved ones who have passed (the creation of an ancestor altar will be covered later in this book). Smoky incense will turn to ash, marking the symbolism of death.

The Web of Your Life

Just as scientists have updated their beliefs about a limited, linear food chain to a more holistic and nonlinear food web, we can update our own beliefs about the past, present, and future of our own lives. We can begin to see them less as a process of acquiring things and gaining accomplishments and more as a vast network of learning, connecting, and growing.

Prepare and gather:

* A large sheet of paper

* Some colored pencils or markers

Begin thinking about the web of your life, with you at the center—just as a spider sits on its own web. Draw a circle that represents you, and then draw lines radiating outward to represent other aspects of your life: the people you love and care about, your work, your commitments and responsibilities, your pets, your hobbies, your spiritual practice, your emotional well-being, and your physical body. Draw small circles at the end of each line, and write the category it represents.

This is the web of your life, so while it may include the categories I list above, you will likely think of others that are specific to you. Let this process take you in any direction it wants, and try to be a witness (not a judge) as you create your personal web on paper.

When your web feels complete, look over what you have written, and marvel at the intricacies, beauty, and complexity of the story of your life. This web is both a work of art on paper and a representation of the work of art that is the story of your life.

Next, consider where you are in terms of balance and cycles within each of these areas. For instance, looking at the web as a whole, are you feeling balance among all the categories? Or are you currently spending too much of your time and energy on one area and not enough in others? Is there anything you can do to change this and come into equilibrium?

Looking at each individual circle, is it balanced within itself or do you want to make changes in this area? For instance, in the circle of your physical body, are you getting enough sleep? Eating nutritious meals? Taking care of your health if you have a medical condition? In terms of your relationships with others, are you making enough time for yourself? Are you renewing your joyful commitments to family and friends? Are you stuck in negative feelings associated with a past relationship?

Looking at the web of your life on paper is a good way to recall that your life is a work of art and you are the artist, as well as a reminder that all of these circles are not you, but simply a part of your story. The real you is the nagual energy that witnesses and creates the story of your life. Take this time to see where you are in the story and what else you want to create or bring balance to, and set your intent in that direction.

Make any notes about the changes you want to make in your journal and date it, and place this work of art on your altar or in your medicine bag. I suggest doing this practice with the change of every season, on or near the equinoxes and solstices, and anytime you want to bring balance, change, and awareness to the art you are creating, the story of your life.

3

THE MEDICINE WHEEL
AND THE MOON

A young woman went to college to learn how to be a set designer for theater and opera productions. In her first year, one professor dedicated a large chunk of class time to having his students paint circles on the floor of the studio. The woman's intrigue about this ongoing assignment quickly gave way to fury. What was she learning? What did this have to do with anything? She made circle after circle of different sizes, desperate to make the "perfect" circle so that she could finally be free from this monotonous task.

After many months, she discovered a method that suited her. She went into a kind of meditative state, churning out the circles with her body while meanwhile traveling deep into her imagination, where she created fantastical visual and emotional worlds.

The professor came and looked at her circles one day and complimented her on them. But she did not respond. He asked her a question. Still nothing. When she came to, still painting circles, the whole class was gathered around her and her work. She looked down, a bit sheepish.

"That's it," her teacher said. "Now you are starting to understand the power of the circle."

One of the most well-known symbols in shamanism is the medicine wheel, a circle with no beginning and no end. For the native peoples of North and South America, the ancient symbol of the medicine wheel has always been an integral part of spiritual life. It contains the cardinal directions of north, south, east, and west. Each direction is traditionally associated with a color, a season, and an element, as well as life cycle stages, family structure, and even ways of thinking. In this way, the medicine wheel is a physical object represented in symbolic artwork, and the image of the wheel is built into landmarks at sacred locations, which are often meeting places for communal ceremonies and rites. The medicine wheel is also an internal idea, a powerful metaphor that guides and brings balance.

Perhaps most importantly, and as the name suggests, a medicine wheel can help facilitate healing. For example, I have a friend who experienced a very deep trauma and awakening in his early twenties. Since childhood, he had been obsessed with and devoted to swimming. From a very young age, his family couldn't keep him out of the water. Soon he was inspired to swim competitively, quickly rising in the ranks as a world-class athlete. Burning with the passion inside him, he spent many long hours in practice and conditioning until, out of the blue, he was in a serious car accident that cost him the use of his legs. His whole world seemed to crumble. He went into a deep depression, no longer able to understand his path or envision his future, but he eventually found a new sense of peace and transformation, and he credits the medicine wheel with this critical change in his perspective.

In a vision, he saw himself standing on a great wheel. He was located on the edge between the east and the south—between fire and water, between child and adolescent. Stretched out before him was a body of water so big he couldn't see to the other side. At first, he recoiled from the water, since it held the memories of his planned life path that he felt was closed to him now. Then he heard a powerful voice urging him toward the water again. As he edged into the coolness of the water, a deep understanding washed over him. The water would hold him, just as he was—with or without the use of his legs. He cried tears of sorrow, acceptance, and finally joy.

The day after his vision, he recommitted to swimming. A new sense of determination surpassed the inspiration that had carried him through his younger years.

In this way, my friend moved from the fire of his early obsession into a phase of fluidity in the water. He experienced a coming of age, moving from child to young adult, and he opened the pathway to a deeper emotional understanding of his circumstances and his capabilities through hard-earned self-acceptance. Using the medicine wheel, he was able to heal from the trauma of his accident and come into the present, just as it was, and set his intent to build from that place.

Just like my friend, the medicine wheel can both heal and guide you in many ways. Let's look at the structure of the medicine wheel and consider what each aspect of the wheel may represent. In the Toltec tradition, life is created by the four elements: fire (*huehueteotl*), water (*tlaloc*), air (*ehecatl*), and earth (*tlalnantzin*). Each of these elements works together, and each is represented in our physical bodies— from the heat we generate in our blood, to the air we breathe, to the water that gives us life and refreshes us, to the earth that makes up our skin and bones.

The medicine wheel represents not only the four elements but also the four cardinal directions, the four seasons, the four stages of life, and the four aspects of the self.

Looking at the chart on the next page, consider how the medicine wheel can be helpful to you in the following situations:

ELEMENT	Wind	Fire	Water	Earth
DIRECTION	North	East	South	West
COLOR	White	Red	Yellow	Black
SEASON	Winter	Spring	Summer	Fall
LIFE STAGE	Elder/ Teacher of Teachers	Child/ Participant	Adolescent/ Student	Adult/ Teacher
ASPECT OF SELF	Mind	Spirit	Emotion	Body

In crisis: When you are in a moment of personal crisis, the wheel can provide both understanding and direction. For instance, where are you on the wheel at this moment with this particular situation? Which direction do you need to go in? Understand that the circle of the wheel holds you and represents not only the cyclical impermanence of all things, but also the welcoming embrace of your community and the wisdom of your ancestors. Use the wheel to give context to your present situation and access your inner wisdom.

Making a decision or taking action: Likewise, when you are considering a big decision about your next step, investigate how it will move your life on the wheel. Will you go from understanding an issue intellectually to feeling it in your heart? Will a steady adult energy give way to childlike wonder? When you understand the phases and transitions in your life in terms of the medicine wheel, it can unlock powerful insights that guide and help you.

In need of healing: Because the wheel is an emblem of all the elements, it is connected to the most powerful healer in the universe—planet Earth and her divine mother energy. When you are experiencing illness or injury in the body or mental suffering, returning to the medicine wheel will support your progress toward healing.

In the next section, we will walk through some ways you can create your own wheel. When you are in need of healing, you can come back to the wheel, and it will give you strength.

I'd like to share with you two ways you can build a medicine wheel. The first will show you how to create a small personal representation of the medicine wheel on paper or another surface as an artistic symbol for your home or altar. The second will explain how to build a larger medicine wheel outdoors that will function as a ceremonial space for you and your community. Once you have created one or both types of wheels, you can perform the ceremony for healing and balance later in this chapter.

Creating a Personal Medicine Wheel

Prepare and gather:

- A large sheet of paper

- Pencils, pens, and any other drawing or artistic medium you enjoy

- A ruler

- A compass for circle drawing (optional)

Begin by drawing a large circle on your paper. This can be any size, but make sure that you leave enough room to add artistic embellishment. A good size would be at least twelve inches in diameter. It doesn't have to be a perfect circle, but you can use a compass or trace an overturned bowl to achieve even proportions. When you've drawn your circle, use your ruler to draw two lines inside the circle, one from top to bottom and the other from side to side. You now have four quadrants within your circle.

Each quadrant represents an element, direction, color, season, life stage, and aspect of self as outlined above. Write the corresponding information in each quadrant using the example below as your guide. If you like, you can use colored pencils or pens in each of the quadrants. Traditional colors for the medicine wheel are usually black, red, white, and yellow, but if

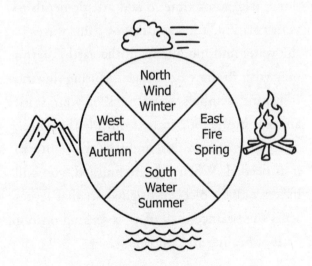

your intuition tells you that green is the color of the earth quadrant for you, then follow your intuition. You can continue to embellish your wheel however your creative spirit moves you.

Instead of paper, you might paint your medicine wheel onto a circular piece of wood, a ceramic plate or platter, or even a large, flat stone. There are many possibilities, so let your creativity be your guide.

Once you have the basic shape and labeling done, take some time to add artistic depth to your creation. You can draw or paint waves in the water and mountains in the earth, or you may wish to draw or collage inspiring illustrations and symbols or pictures of your spirit animals in the four corners outside the wheel. There's no rush to this, and you can return to it as needed. When you are finished, you will have a radiant piece of original art that represents the balance each of us is seeking on our path of healing and wholeness.

When you feel your medicine wheel is complete, place it on your altar or hang it anywhere you will see it regularly, so it can remind you of your spiritual and personal healing goals.

Building an Outdoor Medicine Wheel

Prepare and gather:

- A collection of stones and other natural semipermanent objects

- A compass

- A straight stick or tape measure

First, you need to find a good spot for building your medicine wheel. You may have the resources and space to create a large wheel for your whole community, or you may wish to build a small wheel for ceremony and personal prayer in your backyard, or in the middle of a small garden. These personal wheels can be any size, but I recommend at least three to four feet in diameter so you have enough room to stand in each quadrant.

Clear the area for your medicine wheel by brushing away any debris, leaf litter, or rocks. Also, it's easier to build a medicine wheel on a relatively flat surface that is free of grass.

Once your space is prepared, set a medium-size stone on the ground in the center of where you would like your circle to be. With your compass pointing northwest, set the end of the stick or tape measure down on the middle point of your center stone. Place a marker stone at the other end of your stick. Do this for the other three points: northeast, southwest, and southeast. *Note*: you are marking these mid-points for the lines in your wheel so that when you stand within a quadrant and face outward you will be facing a cardinal direction. See the illustration on the next page for guidance.

When your directional points are marked, use your collection of smaller stones to make straight lines from your center stone to your

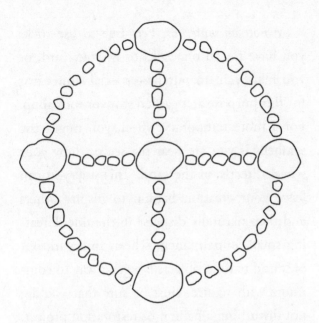

outer marker stones. Stand up and look at your work from a distance on occasion, as this will allow you to better see if your lines are straight or if they need adjustment. You are creating these inner lines first, as it's often easier to build a circle around the lines rather than vice versa. Once you have your center stone and directional lines outlined to your satisfaction, build your circle linking the directional points.

A note on materials: Feel free to use rocks you have found on walks or in your yard, or you may want to purchase special stones just for this purpose at a garden store or rock shop. For a more temporary wheel, you might use seashells if you are near the sea or draw your wheel directly in the sand. This way you can leave your creation behind to inspire others and then naturally disperse in the tide. Creating small, impermanent wheels in a park out of found natural objects is a great way to commune with nature—just be sure that you are not disturbing a habitat or restoration project, blocking a path, or interrupting the natural flow of life around you, and that your creation can be naturally dispersed back to its wild state.

Using Your Medicine Wheel:
A Ceremony for Harmony and Balance

Prepare and gather:

- Your medicine wheel (outside or on paper)

- Your favorite incense (optional)

While a medicine wheel has a variety of ceremonial purposes, I would like to share with you one that can be used to do an inner checkup, to accept the medicinal help of the wheel and recommit yourself to living in harmony and balance. This ceremony uses the traditional Toltec associations with each direction, but feel free to adapt it to fit your own intuitive associations or another tradition if necessary.

To begin, take a moment to center yourself in the present moment. Feel your connection to the earth, and take a few deep, calming breaths. Let go of any anxieties, regrets, fears, or negative thoughts. Light your favorite incense and let its scent calm you and help you focus on the present moment.

With your medicine wheel in front of you (either on the ground or on paper), close your eyes and imagine yourself standing at the top of a great hill. The sky is clear and bright, and the air is crisp and full of the scent of wildflowers and a hint of smoke from a distant bonfire. From the top of the hill you can see far out in all directions, over great plains, farms, and deserts, with mountains in the distance. Take some time to breathe and enjoy this place. It is sacred and exists only for you.

When you are ready, open your eyes and step into the eastern quadrant of the medicine wheel (or place your hand on the eastern quadrant of the medicine wheel you drew on paper). This is the realm of spring and of fire: new beginnings, imagination, passion, creativity, and the spiritual journey. Notice if you feel any resistance in your body or your mind when you are in this quadrant. Have you been neglecting your creative side? Has your spiritual life fallen away due to the obligations of daily life? If so, ask yourself how you might bring these aspects of your life back into balance. Can you work on an artistic project that you've put aside? Do some writing in your journal? Clean and refresh your personal altar?

Close your eyes and imagine that you are back on the hill, looking out over the beautiful valleys to the east. You can feel a warm glow in your solar plexus, radiating out to fill your whole body with powerful, invigorating light. Give thanks for the gifts of creativity, fire, and imagination in your life.

When you are ready, open your eyes, step outside your medicine wheel, and walk around to the southern quadrant (or place your hand in the southern quadrant). The south is the realm of summer and of water, of emotions, mystery, healing, and the life-giving, refreshing properties of the sea, the rivers, and the rain. Ask yourself again if you feel any resistance in your body or your mind here. Are there blocks in your emotional life that need healing? Have you neglected to take time for self-care? If so, spend some time in meditation in this direction, and ask yourself how you might bring these aspects of your life back into balance. Can you take a healing bath? Address some hurt feelings with a friend? Allow yourself to cry over a recent loss?

Close your eyes and return to the hill. Imagine beautiful iron gray clouds gathering above you and releasing a torrent of refreshing rain. Feel it soak into your skin, giving you the power to face your emotions and relax into the natural flow of life. Give thanks for the gifts of tears, laughter, self-care, and all the blessed water in your life.

When the rains have ended and the sky has cleared, open your eyes and walk around the medicine wheel to the western quadrant. The west is the realm of autumn and of earth, of nourishment, groundedness, harvest, the physical body, and the incredible diversity of the living planet. Do you feel any resistance in your body or your mind here? Ask yourself if there are aspects of your physical health that you've been neglecting. Have you been working so hard that you haven't taken the time to enjoy the fruits of all your work? Have you put things in your body that you know do not nourish you? Are there any health issues you need to look into? Spend as much time as you need in this direction, and ask yourself how you might bring these aspects of your life back into balance. Can you take regular walks in a local park or wilderness area to connect to your physical body and the natural world? Is there a meal you can prepare that will nourish your body, mind, and soul? How can you give thanks for the abundant gifts in your life?

Close your eyes and go back to the hill. This time, look down at your feet and their connection to the hill on which you stand. Absorb the strength and power of the Earth and know that, like the trees of the forest or even the smallest wildflower, you are connected to the planet at all times. Give thanks for the gifts of solid foundations, spiritual and physical nourishment, and all fruitful harvests in your life.

When you feel your time in the earth quadrant has come to a natural close, open your eyes and walk around the medicine wheel (or move your hand) to the northern quadrant. The north is the realm of winter and of air, of the mind and all its power, clarity, and the cleansing properties of the rushing wind. Notice again whether you feel any resistance in your body or your mind in this place. Have you felt stagnant and stuck in some particular area of your life? Or perhaps you have been overthinking a particular situation? Alternatively, do you feel you've lost focus or clarity surrounding an issue in your life that you need to bring your mental focus to? Consider these questions deeply and for as long as you need in this direction, and ask yourself how you might bring these aspects of your life back into balance. Can you consider looking at an old problem from a new perspective (or an old argument from the other person's point of view)? Maybe you could explore the mind-clearing practices of mindfulness meditation.

Or, is there someone with more knowledge in a particular area that you could ask for help?

Close your eyes and imagine a sudden gust of wind rushing up the side of the hill to meet you head-on. It is a brisk, bracing wind with a hint of colder climes in it, rich with snow. Imagine any confusion in your mind is blown away as cobwebs in a gale. Give thanks for the gifts of clarity, knowledge, and peace of mind.

When you have walked the medicine wheel around through all four directions, approach the center of the wheel and sit in peaceful, thankful meditation for a few minutes, knowing that whenever your life is out of balance, you can return to this place and be refreshed.

The Power of the Moon

While the sun brings its fiery power to the eastern quadrant of the medicine wheel, we must not forget the other celestial body that appears most often when the sun has made its descent in the west, the moon. Unlike the fierce perpetual burning of its counterpart, the moon changes her face in a regular rhythm we can see from Earth, allowing for cyclical calendar-keeping and affording us the opportunity to honor and celebrate the ever-turning circles and spirals of time in our lives and beyond. The moon's pearly, liquid light is bewitching, and it has captivated the human imagination since time immemorial. There is a physical component to its allure, too. If we remember that its gravitational pull controls the tides of oceans around the world, this leaves little doubt of its ability to influence the 60 percent of our bodies that are made up of water.

In many spiritual traditions, the full moon is a time of celebration and thanksgiving, a time to realize the fulfillment of goals, dreams, and desires. Since the full moon represents the apex of the cycle and the beginning of the waning phase, it is also the perfect time for releasing what no longer serves you emotionally or in other ways, such as old agreements that are holding you back.

Shamanic Full Moon Ceremony

The full moon ceremony that follows is one you can perform that will honor the moon, her mysteries, and the deep cycles of seasonal time. As always, please feel free to adapt this ceremony to make room for your own spiritual traditions. If you have a safe and private natural area you can go to, such as a backyard, it is always powerful to perform this work outside, but if not, don't worry—the moon's potency is not inhibited by human construction.

First, confirm the date of the full moon and choose the space where you can perform your ceremony—outside or inside. If you plan to be outside, then you'll need a surface upon which to place your ceremonial objects. This may be a large stone or even simply a blanket folded up and placed on the ground. You may also do this ceremony inside your home, either at your altar or any place you have a flat surface available.

Prepare and gather:

- Objects representing the four elements:

  - *Air*: a feather or burning incense

  - *Fire*: a lighted candle or small outdoor fire

  - *Water*: a bowl of clean water

  - *Earth*: a sacred stone or bowl of soil or salt

  - *Note*: If your space is small or you don't have access to these items, you can simply draw symbols for these elements on slips of paper.

- A glass of water that you will infuse with the moon's blessing and then drink

- Offerings for the spirits to acknowledge the connection between our human lives and the living world (e.g., cornmeal, sacred dried herbs, bread, oatcakes, milk)

Place all the items you have collected in front of you. When you are ready to begin, take a few deep breaths and allow yourself to come into the present moment.

Close your eyes and imagine a long thread of golden light extending down from your head and through your spine, your legs, and your feet, down into the rich earth, all the way to the center of the planet. Draw strength from this fiery core, and know that at all times you are connected to every other living thing and to the vast and intricate Mother Earth. Now imagine that golden thread moving upward, radiating out from the crown of your head to touch the stars in the night sky. You are simultaneously a being of the physical earth and the heady realm of starlight. There are no past regrets or future anxieties in this place. Feel the wheel of the heavens, the heartbeat of the planet, your guiding spirits seen and unseen, and your breath. Don't rush this important time.

Once you feel grounded to the earth beneath your feet and connected to the stars above, let us open this ceremony with a prayer. I offer one below to be read aloud as a suggestion, but feel free to pray spontaneously from your heart.

Spirits and Powers of the Living World,

Be here with me in this sacred place at this sacred time.

I give thanks for my breath, my body, and my spirit.

Fill my heart with peace, my mind with joy, and my soul with compassion.

Open my eyes so that I may see between the worlds, and honor the silver spirit of Grandmother Moon.

Next we will give thanks to the four elements. Pick up your symbol for each element in turn, and read its corresponding prayer aloud:

Air

*Spirits of the Wind, Wise Ones, Spirits
of Teaching,*

*I honor you and ask you to be with me here
in this sacred time and place.*

*Grant me clarity of vision and the
wisdom of discernment.*

*Let my mind fly like a great bird
toward truth.*

You are welcome here.

Fire

*Spirits of Fire, Laughing Ones, Spirits
of Newness,*

*I honor you and ask you to be with me here
in this sacred time and place.*

Grant me passion of purpose and radiant joy.

*Let my soul dance like a burning flame
toward freedom.*

You are welcome here.

Water

Spirits of Water, Flowing Ones, Spirits of Learning,

I honor you and ask you to be with me here in this sacred time and place.

Grant me the sweetness of flow and emotional balance.

Let my heart leap like a silver fish toward peace.

You are welcome here.

Earth

Spirits of Earth, Grounded Ones, Spirits of Action

I honor you and ask you to be with me here in this sacred time and place.

Grant me the strength of connection and a nourished heart.

Let my hands work in the garden of Being toward abundant kindness.

You are welcome here.

Next, you want to share with the moon what you are grateful for, what you are celebrating, and perhaps what you wish to let go of that is no longer serving you.

When you are ready, raise your glass of water to the moon and imagine that it contains all the hope, goodness, and abundance of this celestial body. Offer it to her as a prayer of thanks, and ask that it be blessed:

> *Grandmother Moon among the stars,*
>
> *Thank you for your radiant light.*
>
> *May I be blessed, may my loved ones be blessed,*
>
> *May all the people and beings in the living world be blessed.*

Drink the glass of water while imagining your life filled with the abundant blessings of the full moon. Any water left over can be poured out as an offering.

When you feel your ceremony drawing to a close, give thanks to each of the spirits you invited into your space—whatever guiding spirits you invoked as well as those of the elements of air, fire, water, and earth. Leave small offerings of cornmeal or herbs in each of the four directions.

4

ANIMAL WISDOM

I have four little dogs at home, and one thing I love is that no matter what challenges I am experiencing in my Personal Dream, when I walk in the front door they are always happy to see me. They share their love with me no matter what. Every time I experience this, I am reminded of this profound difference between humans and the rest of the animal world.

As mentioned earlier, humans have a mind that is constantly dreaming, and for so many of those who live their lives unconsciously, the mind overflows with regrets of the past, fears of the future, or negative judgments of the present. Unlike humans, animals live only in the present moment. They don't tell stories to themselves about how they are not good enough or worry that they might never find true love. So even though they may experience challenges and a range of emotions, animals don't create problems for themselves via a dreaming mind.

To be clear, the dreaming of the human mind has given us incredible gifts too, such as the ability to imagine and create everything from language to architecture, art to theoretical physics. So our goal here is to enrich these helpful aspects of the dreaming mind, while becoming aware of and detaching from the unhelpful stories we tell ourselves.

Whenever the shamans in my family noticed themselves or someone else getting caught in the nightmare of the storytelling mind, they would point to the animals for guidance about living free in the present moment. The shamans understood that life only exists in the present moment, where the nagual is. The mind's addiction to suffering very often pulls us out of the present moment to seek peace in the future, as when we think we will be happy only when we acquire this or achieve that. The irony is that this very act of seeking peace prevents us from finding it. The only place where peace truly exists is the here and now. One of the greatest lessons we can learn from our fellow animal beings is this importance of living in the present moment.

The idea that we can learn from animals is contrary to other spiritual and cultural worldviews, especially those that propose a dualistic split in human nature. They posit that there is a spiritual and a material world and within human beings there likewise is a "spiritual side" and a "physical side" to our lives. From this perspective, the spiritual side is described as "higher," and the material world or physical side is equated with the body and often designated as "lower." In many traditions, this "lower" aspect of life is called the "animal" side of humanity. Implicit in this idea is that animals and animal traits are inherently less-than, while human beings are "superior." Some traditions have gone even further and declared that animals were created to be of service to us, that lands sit waiting to be claimed by humans, and that the whole natural world exists for our pleasure and profit.

The Toltec tradition embraces a totally different worldview. We don't split the material and the spiritual world. Why would we? Everywhere I look, and everything I see, pulses with the nagual, the force that gives life to all things. For a monotheist, I would say that "it is all the mind of God." For us, physical and spiritual reality is all one: encompassed in the Dream of the Planet, which is our own creation.

The Toltec tradition teaches that animals are our brothers and sisters on this planet and we have much to learn from them. Learning from the animal world begins by noticing any of your own beliefs about being superior to animals. Certainly, there are differences between us and animals, and the thinking mind has given us the immense gifts of communication and creation, but in order to awaken fully to the Dream of the Planet and our part in it, we must understand ourselves within nature and the animal world. We are part of a larger whole, not rulers over some imaginary natural kingdom.

The moment we stop seeing ourselves as superior to animals is the moment we open ourselves to learn from them. For instance, think about a dog. What can you learn from this beautiful creature? In addition to the great lesson of living in the present moment, the dog offers the gifts of loyalty and enthusiasm, as well as the importance of incorporating play and rest into every day. There are valuable lessons for us in these traits.

In another example, consider what you may learn from the ants. Notice how, despite their tiny size, they work together in harmony to build incredible structures that are one hundred, one thousand, or even ten thousand times the size of any one individual ant. They possess the gifts of cooperation, tenacity, and achievement for the benefit of the common good. They exemplify the idea that any goal can be broken down into the smallest, most doable actions. What might you achieve in your life, ant-like step after ant-like step, with the help of your community?

When we think of animal wisdom, we can draw on images of iconic wild animals like the bobcat, coyote, eagle, or bear. But even daily sightings and interactions with local animals and our pets provide reminders to live in the moment instead of living in our heads. Simply observing an animal, any animal, can serve as a reminder to move into the present moment, which is a crucial step in waking up to the Dream of the Planet. This is one of the reasons that animals figure so strongly in shamanic storytelling: by emphasizing an animal's attributes through the art of story, we can pass on the importance of these gifts and the power of adopting them ourselves in pursuit of creating our own dream.

There are a number of practices you can cultivate that will increase your awareness regarding the great diversity of gifts the animal world has to offer. The following practices include conscious observation, developing a special relationship with a specific spirit animal, and "stalking the self" through a powerful inner journey with your spirit animal.

Observing the Gifts of the Animals

Prepare and gather:

- A notebook and a pen

- Music for meditation and focus (optional)

One way to learn from animals is to simply be with and observe them. You can do this at any time and at a moment's notice, but I suggest that you begin this work by setting aside a specific time to do so and allowing at least fifteen minutes to fully engage with the practice. Being in the presence of animals is always powerful, and there are also vast libraries of raw footage online featuring animals from all over the world. You can perform this act of conscious observation with any animal, from the smallest to the largest. You can observe the insect that crawls across your floor, your dog or cat, the squirrels or birds in your yard, or, if you're in a rural area, the cows or horses in the fields. You may also have the opportunity to observe a wild animal while on a hike in the wilderness; just be sure to think of your own safety as well as the habitat needs of the animal and its surroundings. These encounters can be thrilling, but don't discount the everyday animals in our midst, and even those that many people fear or avoid, like rats, mice, raccoons, possums, bats, and snakes. Remember the old saying, "If you think you are too small to make a difference, try going to bed with a mosquito." All animals have something to teach if we are willing to learn.

Begin by settling into your space. Let go of any past fears or anxieties. Let your mind settle into a receptive, watchful state; if it helps you to listen to music in order to quiet your mind, try to do so on a set of earbuds or headphones so the noise doesn't frighten away any animal life. Take a deep breath. You may wish to spend some time with your eyes closed, imagining yourself to be a tree, rock, or other part of the landscape. This helps to send an energetic message to the animals in the area that you are a friendly observer only and not a threat.

If you are in nature, allow some time for an animal to arrive in your general vicinity. Welcome all animals as honored visitors from the living world; don't be disappointed if you only see animals you run into every day, like squirrels, bees, or pigeons. These hardy creatures have much to teach, such as the gift of adaptation.

As you observe the animal, see if you can bring to mind any associations you may already have with that creature. There may be mythological, religious, or cultural stories built over generations of animal observation that can tell us something about the gifts these animals have offered to our ancestors and which may still have meaning for us today.

Consider how these gifts may help you in your personal life. How might your inner self, your healing journey, and your community benefit from the swift darting movement of the garter snake, the unceasing song of the cicada, or the conserving hibernation of the hedgehog or the bear?

Make it a point in all of your observations to note the presence and grace that each animal has within it, without the dreaming mind and its addiction to suffering.

Once you have spent some time in conscious observation with an animal and have considered the gifts it offers, you may wish to go further and imagine that you are able to move your consciousness into its body and see through its eyes. What does the world like from its perspective? Notice the moment to moment aliveness to the present circumstances, without getting tripped up in the past or future. Step into the mind of the animal you are watching. That idea may seem strange, that you can place your own mind inside another being, but in Toltec shamanism we don't believe consciousness is confined to the mind or body. That is to say, it's not localized in the brain. This allows the shaman to "reach out" with consciousness and communicate with the living world in a more profound way, enabling each of us to see through the eyes of our brother and sister animals, as well as plants, rivers, mountains, and the planet.

When your observations come to a close, say a short "thank you" to the animal for the lessons it has to teach and for spending time with you on this day. You may want to leave a small offering of seeds or other animal food as a way to express your gratitude. Take some time to write your observations and notes in your journal.

Spirit Animals

In the Toltec tradition (as well as many other shamanic cultures), we teach about the importance of spirit animals. You may have encountered material about spirit animals before; sometimes they are referred to as power animals or totem animals. While some cultures differ in their approach to these special animal guides and companions, the terms are similar.

Some traditions believe that the shaman must wait for an animal to appear in dreams or journeys, or in the midst of a specific ceremony. In the Toltec tradition, we believe that you choose your spirit animals based on the work you've done in discerning the gifts and qualities you most wish to cultivate in yourself. You can see why it's critical to spend time with the previous exercise in animal observation before initiating these sacred relationships. When you choose a particular animal or animals because you are drawn by certain characteristics, you can bring those very qualities into your Personal Dream to use as tools. At any time, for example, we can be as strategic as the eagle, as cunning as the fox, or as powerful as the jaguar.

I recommend choosing three animal spirit guides. In my own life, I have chosen the bat, the rattlesnake, and the jaguar as my spirit animals. The bat came to me when I was learning how to move through the world after being temporarily blinded due to a physical illness. Without the benefit of sight, I had to learn a whole new way of being. This also showed me that I needed to learn how to bypass my mind and follow my heart and intuition instead—this was the gift I received from the bat, and something I still call on to this day when I feel lost. The bat has given me a way to hone in on my own inner guidance while being blind to whatever outside glimmers might distract or tempt me.

I am also connected to the rattlesnake. As babies, rattlesnakes cannot control their venom, and at one time I was that way with my emotional venom. When I was upset, I would "bite" whoever came near me, no matter what their intentions, and I would release all my venom at once. But I matured as a rattlesnake does; I became aware of my venom and learned to control it.

My third spirit animal is the jaguar. The jaguar hunts by stalking and embodies action in the moment. The jaguar holds intent and force and power. I call on the spirit of the jaguar when I need to move forward, when my doubts and fears would rather keep me locked up and passive. When I call on this incredibly powerful animal, I remind myself that I am powerful with my intent, and I can manifest my own desires, dreams, and goals if I take the actions required.

Everyone is capable of establishing this special relationship with a spirit animal. You may already have an animal (or two or three) that you know is an important part of your life or that seems to appear regularly in your dreams or in everyday life. Some people developed an interest in a specific animal as a child or receive regular gifts related to a specific animal. These may be signs that you have subconsciously chosen your spirit animals. However, don't feel bound to choose something that others associate with you. Leave room to be drawn to a particular animal, or an attribute you'd like to cultivate, regardless of what others may think. This is your journey.

Finding Your Spirit Animals

Prepare and gather:

- A pen and journal

To begin this practice, settle into a quiet place and do a silent meditation for at least five minutes, but more if you feel so moved. Quiet the mind and focus on your breath during this period, settling down from the constant motion of the world.

When you feel calm and relaxed, read the following prayer/mantra out loud:

Animal Spirits, Allies and Guides,

Friends of feather, fur, and claw,

I open my heart and seek your wisdom.

Teachers of the living world,

You are welcome here.

When your prayer is complete, write down the animals that enter into your mind.

I encourage you to do this all at once without limiting or editing your thoughts—animals may come through that you don't expect. Then review your list and write down all the qualities each animal represents for you. Here are a few examples to get you started:

Butterfly: Transformation, glamour

Cat: Independence, discernment

Eagle: Strategy, leadership

Earthworm: Renewal, groundedness

Elephant: Maternal and family energy, gentle power

Horse: Strength, sensitivity to others

Lizard: Fast reflexes, primal instincts

Rabbit: Creative sexual energy, self-protection

Shark: Ferocity, survival, sixth sense

Snake: Cunning, emotional power

Squirrel: Observation, readiness

Tortoise: Determination, steadiness

Whale: Ancient wisdom, migration

Woodpecker: Curiosity, diligence

Remember: the qualities listed here are what these animals represent to me—but what's important is what the animals represent to *you*. The path of the shaman is about following your own truth, and yours will be different from mine.

After you've made your list, contemplate each animal and its attributes, and then pick three that have traits you currently see or want to cultivate within yourself.

After you have made your selections, close the ceremony by thanking the animals for coming to you in this way. Over the next few days, find a symbol representing each of your three animals for your personal altar or medicine bag. This could be a feather you find on the ground, some of the animal's hair, a small statue, or even a photo of the animal.

Start calling in your spirit animals when you need their gifts to manifest during your day. For example, if you are struggling to make a big change in your life, call on the power of the butterfly to transform. If you are hoping to expand your family, ask the rabbit for her blessings. After a month or two of regularly calling on your spirit animals, return to your list and write down any new qualities you have discovered in your time working with them.

Stalking the Self: A Journey with Your Spirit Animal

For this exercise, you'll focus on one animal spirit only. To start, find a safe, comfortable space where you can be free from interruption for at least thirty minutes. Sit in a comfortable chair with your feet flat on the ground, connecting you to Mother Earth.

Center yourself by taking a few deep, calming breaths. Let go of any anxieties about the future or worries from the past—there is only you in this space at this perfect time.

Close your eyes, and picture in your mind your spirit animal. If you have an established way of contacting your animal, such as going to a specific place in the inner world to meet them, please do so. When I say "inner world," I mean whatever version of your imaginative consciousness comes up for you in meditation, prayer, or a dream state. In this space, see your animal in front of you and be filled with the joy and peace of being in the presence of this powerful, loving ally.

Look into the eyes of your spirit animal—notice how they differ from your human eyes. They may be piercing, like the eyes of a bird of prey, or deep liquid pools like those of an otter. See them move toward you until their eyes are right in front of you. Now imagine you close your eyes in the inner world, and when you open them, you are no longer looking at the eyes of your spirit animal; you are looking through them. Look around at the inner world through the eyes of this amazing creature. What is it like to see with the eyes of your spirit animal? What do you notice that you may not have noticed before? Explore the landscape that fills the inner mind as you travel in your animal's consciousness, whether it's jungle, desert, ocean, or grassy backyard.

You may also wish to view a part of your human life with the eyes of your spirit animal. This can be a very powerful experience. Think of a time and place in your life you would like to visit; this could be a happy occasion or a difficult time. What does looking at this event through the eyes of your animal reveal to you? What qualities does your animal offer you that you might not have had on your own? (Note: If you become too emotionally involved in the scene, you may realize that you are no longer seeing through the eyes of your spirit animal. Simply take some deep, cleansing breaths and return to your animal.)

Revisiting your human experience in the body of your spirit animal allows you to do what some shamans call "stalking the self," and it can lead to powerful revelations and personal healing. Know that in every moment, you are protected by your spirit animal. Together with this ally you can guide yourself out of your own negative stories and see the truth of your life.

When you are ready, close your eyes in the inner world, and when you open them you will be seeing through your own eyes and looking once again into the face of your beloved friend. Thank it for its help and guidance, and ask if there are any additional messages for you at this time.

Once you have said goodbye, return to your body in the living world. Take several deep breaths and stretch your arms and legs.

Wiggle your toes and fingers. When ready, open your eyes and return completely to this space at this time.

I recommend that you spend some time immediately after this exercise recording your experiences in a journal so you can be sure to capture the details of the experience and return to them later for further reflection.

5

POWER OBJECTS

A woman hikes up a hill in a local park in the early morning hours just before sunrise. She carries a backpack and a walking stick that she uses to steady her feet and clear away sharp rocks from the path. She arrives at her special spot on top of the hill just as the sun rises over the valley. She can see the skyscrapers and other tall buildings downtown in the distance. She sets her backpack on the ground and pulls out an old felt pouch—opening it, she removes a gnarled piece of driftwood wrapped in different colored ribbons, a chunk of black tourmaline, a tiny seashell wrapped gently in a small piece of tissue paper, a number of acorns strung together with a thin blue cord, and a hand-made rattle from a gourd she grew the previous year in her garden for that purpose. She places the acorns around her neck, takes the black stone in one hand and the rattle in the other, and begins to pray for the people of her city: for all who are rising to begin their workday, for those who wake with worries and doubts already in their minds, for those with bills to pay and children to feed.

▲▽▲▽▲▽▲

As this beautiful story illustrates, material objects in the Dream of the Planet can be powerful tools to help us align our intentions with love instead of fear, to be of service to others and to Mother Earth. They can also serve as physical representations or reminders of goals we have or qualities we want to cultivate within ourselves.

When material objects take on these roles, we call them power objects. A power object, or totem, is a sacred object or symbol with which you create a personal relationship so that you can call upon its power and everything it represents.

From a shamanic perspective, rather than being mere lifeless "things," all objects in the Dream of the Planet contain nagual energy. Even Western science has recognized this within the last century, teaching that everything on this beautiful planet is made up of atoms, whose particles are in constant motion. So when you look at a rock, a stick, or any other object that appears "lifeless," the reality is that it is made up of tiny little particles that are moving all the time. Energy, or nagual, makes matter possible.

You have undoubtedly experienced the energy of certain objects many times in your life, even if you didn't name it as such at the time. For instance, if you have ever felt drawn to an object, whether in nature or at a store, the energy within the object often accounts for your attraction to it. When seen this way, we begin to understand the vibrational relationship between our own energy and that of certain objects; we just refer to this more commonly as "I like this" and "I don't like this." While likes and dislikes can certainly be based on the dreaming mind, we can be led by instinct to deep energetic affinities. This is especially true when we say things like, "I like this, and I'm not sure why."

Of course, when our internal medicine bag is filled with tools of negativity and we are unaware of it, we can be drawn to objects that feed that negative energy and create suffering in our lives. You can often see this best in hindsight, when you look back and realize you were drawn to something that you now see as unhelpful or even self-destructive (alcohol and drug abuse would be examples of this). When you clean out your internal medicine bag, you often find that the things you were once drawn to no longer appeal to you anymore. You may also notice that when you have a "bad day," which means you get caught in the addiction to suffering as we all do from time to time, you are once again tempted by or drawn to these destructive elements.

Once you are able to recognize the energy of objects and understand how some of them have a special appeal for you, you can learn how to use them in a positive way as tools to help you on your path. You can call on their power and even amplify it in order to pull your heart and mind into alignment with the nagual. When you form a special bond with an object or when you add to it with your own creativity and artistic skills, the power of the object is amplified, and it can help you move further along the path you desire.

Many of us already have objects that resonate with us, but perhaps we haven't identified them as power objects just yet. Doing so can transform these items from special to sacred and increase our energetic connection with them. I will explain a ceremony to help you do just that.

Power Object Ceremony

Prepare and gather:

- A collection of three to five items that have personal significance to you

- Your favorite incense (optional)

The first step is to think about the objects you have now that already hold a special place in your heart. For instance, perhaps you have a rock, shell, piece of jewelry, religious icon, coin, or small gift you treasure. Once you have identified certain objects with which you feel a special connection, the next step is to go deeper into what these objects symbolize for you.

Consider each object's significance. For instance, if it was given to you as a gift, perhaps it symbolizes friendship, connection, or love. If it's something collected while on vacation, it may symbolize peace, adventure, or the need to relax. If it's a religious icon, maybe it reminds you to have faith that everything is happening just as it should, even when it appears otherwise.

Once you have identified the objects and thought about the qualities that they hold for you, add a special dedication ceremony for them.

Taking the first object in your hand, think of the qualities that it holds. Using your consciousness, direct your intent into the object. Your intent can begin transforming your special object into an amplified and potent symbol of the positive qualities it already stands for. Close your eyes and visualize your intent flowing from your body into the power object. Imagine that your intent takes a firm hold within the object, like roots in rich, fertile soil. Say the following prayer out loud, inserting the quality or qualities the object can help activate within you:

> *Thank you for coming to me. I understand that you are a symbol for _____. I set my intent on this, and when I need to cultivate _____, I ask that you help me. Every time I see or think of you, I will remember my intent to have _____ in my life.*

Once you have done this, you may want to put this object in your medicine bag or on your personal altar. If it already has a special place in your home, perhaps keep it there. Every time you see it now, it will remind you of the qualities you are trying to cultivate within yourself, and it will send this energy to you. You may also call on your sacred items in times of need, even holding one in your hand if it is with you, to strengthen your resolve.

A Power Object Walk

Prepare and gather:

- A pair of scissors or a small knife to clip flowers or branches (make sure that gathering these items is permitted in your area, and that they are safe to handle)

- A bag or basket for items that call to you on your journey

- A map of the area for recording where you found a specific item (optional)

Power objects will make themselves known to you at the right time, but you must be available so they can find you. One of the best ways to do this is to take regular walks in nature. Remember, the living world does not end at the boundaries of a town or city, and even in a busy downtown area you might be surprised by what comes to you.

As you walk, open your heart and mind to the living world. Be aware of your surroundings and let your senses guide you. The scent of a blooming plum tree or the sound of moving water could be an invitation to investigate further. When you do arrive at a spot where you feel you have been drawn, look around and see if there is an object that calls to you. If you find one, pick it up and ask if it is willing to come with you and become part of your spiritual path. Feel its energy in your hand, and see if any images immediately spring to mind.

How you interpret the object's response is a matter of personal intuition; but if you have any doubts, thank the object and set it back where it came from. Whether or not the object comes with you, you can be thankful to nature for its guidance.

Be sure to take your time with this process. You are creating relationships with objects just by walking through the living world with an open heart. Don't expect that you will come back from every walk with a sacred object—these are incredibly special items, and it may take several outings in different places before you find an item that truly calls to you.

Once you've found an object, perform the dedication ceremony covered on page 102. You can then add this power object to your medicine bag or personal altar.

Artful Power Objects

Lastly, because Toltec shamanism recognizes the importance of life as art, I see virtually all physical art as power objects. In most cases, the artist has taken materials and combined them with their sincere intent, skill, and energy to create something new and beautiful. In this way, art contains a combination of the energy of the objects and the energy of the artist—and because we are all unique expressions of the energy of life, we each resonate with different artists or pieces.

For this reason, any art that you create can be a power object if you'd like it to be. This is especially true for anyone who has ever said,

"I'm not creative." Every human is creative. As children, we were all creative—drawing pictures, playing make-believe, telling stories—but at some point we were told or decided that we weren't "real" artists or that our art wasn't "good enough."

Creating a painting, sculpture, craft, or poem—all of these help free the mind from the old story of "I'm not creative." You can perform the sacred object dedication ceremony with any art you create to make it a power object for you too, then place it on your altar or inside your medicine bag.

In addition, you can decorate one of your existing power objects, as this can serve the dual purpose of magnifying the intent you put in the object and reminding yourself that you are a powerful creator. For instance, you could decorate and embellish an object with ribbons, paint, stones, dried flowers, or feathers. This will not only heighten the beauty of your object but also deepen your relationship with it, while activating the creator inside you in the process.

If you feel called to embellish one of your power objects or incorporate it into a piece of art, you can begin by holding the object and opening to the idea that it might show you what it wants to be. Michelangelo described being able to see into a block of marble to the figure inside and said that his work was only to take away everything that was not the sculpture.

In this way, use your intuitive mind and stay open to suggestions from the living world or the object itself. There are a variety of ways to decorate an object beyond traditional means— you could use small feathers left on the ground by passing birds, shiny pebbles or stones, nuts and seeds, or dried leaves and flowers. You could submerge the object in a jar full of water or oil or place it inside a special glass box. The possibilities are endless.

As you create your art, you can add to the sacredness of the process by burning some incense or smudge sticks while you work or cleansing the space with water or sound (chanting, playing a drum or rattle, listening to sacred music). This can be a creative ceremony in its own right. Ask the spirits to guide your hands as you work, and remember, don't be afraid to try something new. That is the point of creativity—to do something you haven't done before and make that which is familiar feel new.

As we come to the end of this chapter, you have likely realized that a power object can work to solidify a new agreement with yourself. Imagine you're like the woman at the beginning of this chapter, standing on a high hill and reaching into a bag full of beautiful objects that vibrate with intent and meaning. Hold the vision of your own medicine bag, well loved and tended, ever evolving, supporting your greatest wish. Now imagine using your sacred objects in ceremonies that serve, protect, expand, and nurture your creative, positive additions to the Dream of the Planet.

6

HONORING THE ANCESTORS

At the end of a devastating war, a baby boy was found on the doorstep of an orphanage. A note pinned to his clothes gave his first name and date of birth but offered no other information. This boy was adopted by a family in another country on the opposite side of the world. Though his siblings and parents doted on him and loved him dearly, he always felt the wound of separation. As an adult, he journeyed to the country of his birth—to the very step on which he was found as a baby. Once he got there, he dissolved into tears. Hunched over, he didn't notice an elderly woman approach him. She sat next to him on the step and touched his shoulder gently. He raised his head and looked deeply into her eyes.

"You will never be a stranger," she said. "For anywhere that you go, the ancestors guide and protect you."

"But I lost them," he cried. "They don't even know who I am."

"Not possible," she replied. "Though you do not know them by sight or have memories and photos, they nonetheless live on inside you. How could it be any other way? They are in your heart."

With that, she touched his chest with her fingertips, rose, and shuffled away.

▲▽▲▽▲▽

In my tradition, as in many other shamanic traditions, we place great importance on honoring our ancestors. Just as nature and the animal world show us that we are connected to all life, when we honor those who came before us, we take our place as part of a great, unending procession that has no beginning and no end. This is the nagual. When we remember our parents, grandparents, and beyond, we see that they are all in a massive flow of energy and life, still moving through us now. We are the flower of their lives, and the seed for the lives that will come after us.

Furthermore, consider the idea that your ancestors are not only those to which you are related biologically. You may feel that you have ancestors of spirit, people whose art or philosophies have influenced you or helped you find healing on your journey through life. Your "ancestors," therefore, could be biological, artistic, spiritual, or all of the above. No matter who they are, they embody the beliefs, traditions, and stories that came before you, that forged the path that brought you to this planet. By remembering and honoring your ancestors, you bring awareness of their wisdom into your life and embody it for yourself in the present moment. Their energy, their dreams, and their love can continue to live through you.

What the man in the story at the beginning of this chapter did not know is that he can always call on his ancestors when he needs them, for they are never far away. When should you call on your ancestors? In addition to the everyday blessings of remembering your ancestors, they can also be called on as powerful allies in moments of difficulty or when facing a hard decision. Talking to your ancestors can bring clarity in raising your own children or helping care for elders. You can also draw on your relationships with your ancestors for the pure joy and gratitude they give you or for inspiration and strength as you set out on new ventures.

Sometimes you will find that your ancestors will speak to you, and you only have to open your awareness to their presence to hear them. Whether or not you believe in ghosts or spirits, you can certainly incorporate the medicine of powerful *remembrance* that comes to you on an intuitive level. For example, maybe your uncle was a trickster, so when something goes missing or your shoe comes mysteriously untied, you remember his mischievous spirit and how he taught you to laugh and be open to joy. Perhaps your mother loved elephants, so you know when you see one that this is an invitation to say hello to her and to thank her for the gifts she brought to your life. I have one friend who acknowledges the presence of a beloved friend who passed every time a light flickers or burns out.

Of course, when death comes as a surprise, as it sometimes does, there may be unresolved energy that you want to express. For instance, I have a friend whose father died suddenly and unexpectedly of a heart attack when she was a teenager. He was a relatively young and healthy man, and nothing could have prepared his loved ones for the shock. To make matters worse, the girl became obsessed with remembering her last words to her father before he died. It had been their habit to always say "I love you" whenever they said goodbye on the phone or in person. The last morning she saw him, however, they had been arguing. She was running late for school and had asked him for a ride, which would make him late to work, and she couldn't remember whether they had said "I love you" when she got out of the car. She knew that their love was very deep. He was a devoted father and teacher, loving and wise, and she adored and respected him deeply. But in the pain and immediacy of the loss, whether she had said "I love you" that morning became an all-consuming question for her.

After he died, she began to sleep day and night and had difficulty eating. Her skin became ashen, she lost weight, and there were dark circles under her eyes. Grief was overtaking her body and her spirit.

Though she had no formal training in creating altars or rituals, she found herself doing just that. Each day, she would walk from her house into the big city park nearby, going off the trails and into the wooded areas where there were no people or any sign of the city. She soon found a spot where she felt the presence of her father. Being there brought on waves of emotion. She was able to be alone there, sometimes weeping and sometimes laughing with memories and thoughts, sometimes imagining conversations with him. Still, the question plagued her. Had she said "I love you"?

One day, she began to gather small sticks and branches in the park. She cleared a little patch of forest floor and arranged the pieces into a message. She spelled out the words I LOVE YOU and then surrounded them with an oval of sticks, branches, and leaves. Making the words physical in this place where she felt her father's presence opened a door in her heart. For the first time, she experienced a small bit of relief.

Each day she visited the message, at first tending and repairing it after rain or wind damaged it, but later stopping by less frequently and intentionally leaving the message to naturally decay and dissipate on the forest floor.

Years later, she returned to the place again. There were no physical signs of her message remaining, but she still felt the power of her love and loss. The message "I love you" whispered through the branches in the wind, rustled in the undergrowth, and crunched under her feet as she walked. It was then that she knew she did not have to worry about this question any longer and that her worry had been just another way to keep her mind obsessed with grief and suffering, a kind of waking death. There was never any question of her love for her father or his for her. In fact, she realized that her suffering was a great dishonor to her father. She could never truly honor him by trying to hold herself back from living her life. Only truly living could give his memory the respect and love it deserved. She felt his love as a profound gift in her life, and she was grateful.

My friend's powerful realization—that it is only through living our best lives that we can do the greatest honor and service to our loved ones who have passed on—is in fact a Toltec teaching. In the Toltec tradition, the deeper purpose of the Day of the Dead, celebrated November 2, isn't to celebrate loved ones who have passed away, but rather to remind ourselves of the ways in which we are dead even as we are living. It is a wake-up call. Our suffering is a way to run and hide from life, and we can imagine our deceased loved ones shaking us, saying "Hey! You're alive! Wake up and celebrate life! Really live!" In this way, we get an invitation to come back to life, to be resurrected ourselves. I believe in resurrection in this life, that when we commit to ending our mind's addiction to suffering we can live differently—we can start being who we are and come alive once more.

One way to cultivate the medicine of remembrance is through a blessed keepsake. This may be an item that you find in the natural world, one that you create, or one that you inherited from a loved one. For example, a friend has a watch that belonged to his father before he passed away which has been a source of comfort and strength for him over the years. Through the power of memory and presence, this watch offers my friend a way to connect to his father when he needs guidance and support. He keeps it in his medicine bag and pulls it out whenever he needs to call on his father's strength or wants to ask for his help in making a decision. A blessed keepsake serves as a bridge between the present and the past, between the visible and invisible worlds.

Blessed Keepsake Ceremony

The following ceremony can be used to create a new blessed keepsake or amplify the power of one that you may already keep with you.

Prepare and gather:

- A glass of water or a plate of your ancestor's favorite foods

- A small candle

- Your favorite incense or a scent your ancestor especially liked (optional)

- Music your ancestor especially liked (optional)

- An item of special significance that reminds you of a beloved ancestor (a piece of jewelry, a lucky coin, a military medal, a paintbrush, a seashell)

This ceremony can be performed at your personal altar or anywhere with a table. (We often have strong memories of family in our kitchens, so a kitchen table might be a great place for this.) Set your glass of water or plate of food out on the table, light your candle to signal to the spirit world your intention, light your incense (or spray a small amount of perfume in the air), and play any special music you've selected. You are creating the bridge between the present and the past we discussed earlier, and the intent generated by these familiar, resonant sights, smells, and sounds will help you infuse your keepsake with memory.

Hold your chosen keepsake in your hand and imagine that you are inviting your ancestor to come have a bite and visit. See the face of your ancestor in your mind and open your heart to allow yourself to sense their presence. Now, think of a strong memory that you associate with your loved one—an event you attended together, a funny story, or a trait or characteristic that you always associate with them. When you are ready, tell this story out loud, as though you are talking to your ancestor, saying, "I remember when . . ." or "Whenever I see _____, I think of you."

Imagine that all of these memories and feelings, sights, sounds, and smells are combining into a great, multicolored light in the room. See that light as it surrounds and is drawn into the keepsake in your hands until the object is glowing with memory and presence. Take your time. This can be an emotional experience; allow your body to go with the flow and let your feelings come and go. If you have more stories and memories you want to tell, do so.

When you feel ready, end your ceremony by expressing love and gratitude to your ancestor for the gifts they have given you. Let them know that you accept the blessing of having known them and that you will take that blessing out into the world by living your life as best you know how.

Your keepsake is now blessed and imbued with the memories and love you give to and receive from your ancestor. Know that whenever you need strength or guidance, you can hold your blessed keepsake in your hands and be in the presence of your loved one. This keepsake is now ready for your medicine bag, personal altar, or ancestral altar or to be kept in any special place that feels right to you.

Your Ancestral Altar

Another powerful way to honor your ancestors is by creating an altar for them. Your ancestor altar can be a place to leave gifts for your ancestors during specific holidays such as Dia de los Muertos (or other holidays of significance to your family, such as your ancestors' birthdays), or it may be a place where you can simply spend time with them and honor their memory. Here are some guidelines and suggestions for creating your own sacred space in which to honor your ancestors. Remember, this can include your ancestors of spirit as well as your biological ancestors.

Prepare and gather:

- Photos, paintings, or drawings of your ancestors

- Belongings precious to the deceased, such as jewelry, keepsakes, lucky tokens, perfume, or books

- Religious or spiritual iconography that was important to them or that holds meaning for you

- Symbols from nature or life that the person loved or cherished

- Flowers, sweets, food, alcohol, or money to symbolize the energy/gifts your ancestors enjoyed in life

- Candles and incense

Honoring our ancestors and thinking about death remind us to wake up from death and start living again. This is the gift of remembrance—a reminder that resurrection is available to us within our lives and that we can be fully present to each day. For this reason, and because you are the artist of your own life, as always I encourage you to make this altar your own. In this way, you will be able to create and maintain an altar that not only honors and gives thanks for your loved ones who have passed, but also serves as a daily reminder to make sure you yourself are truly alive.

Set up your altar in any way that feels festive, joyful, and lovely to you. Remember, the point here is to celebrate life, not to dwell in the negative and painful aspects of death—so feel free to make your altar as colorful, bright, and energetic as you wish.

Once your altar is arranged, try to make it a habit to stop at your altar and catch up with your loved ones regularly. This might take the form of chatting with them out loud, thinking warm and loving thoughts, or imagining white light around them and yourself. It can also take the form of asking questions or requesting assistance (the responses to which may surprise you by coming up in mysterious ways throughout your day or in your dream states). If you have placed any fresh flowers or perishable food on your ancestor altar, be sure to check regularly to make sure you are taking away spoiled items and replacing them with fresh ones.

You can also use this time to speak to yourself in the way that a loving grandparent might. This is especially helpful if you are going through a difficult time or having trouble seeing beyond the limited view of shame or self-doubt. Speak to yourself as a beloved descendant. Tell yourself that all of your experiences up to this point are important and you are exactly where you are supposed to be. Acknowledge out loud that all the struggles you are facing are actually a huge pile of rich, golden life experience, even if you can't see it yet. Remind yourself that you are loved. You are the product of generations of love, and you hold the capacity to carry that love to future generations. You can also give your shoulders a shake and remind yourself to "Wake up!" and celebrate living.

7

DIVINATION TOOLS AND CEREMONIAL PRACTICES

One day, a young boy found himself bored and restless, and he asked his mother what he should do. "Whatever you like, my sweet," she said. Not satisfied with her answer, he found his father. "You should get to work, my love," he said. The boy moved through the house with quick steps, his mind raced, but still he was bored and restless. Then he found himself in front of an old-fashioned radio in the family's living room. He fiddled with the dials and turned it on. One station played unruly jazz. Another was heavy metal, filling his head with its sonic power. He kept turning the dial, looking for something. And then he found it. This music was like nothing he'd ever heard. His body swayed, his shoulders dropped, and when his parents came to the door of the living room to peer in on him, they saw him in the middle of a free-spirited dance. From the old-fashioned radio, however, came only gentle static—the boy danced with joy and purpose to the music in his heart.

▲▼▲▼▲▼

In the Toltec tradition, we say that the wisdom you seek is inside you. This means that whatever answers you need can always be found deep within your truest self. That being said, we sometimes need help in finding the answers within, turning up the volume of our own music. We all need to reach out and seek guidance from time to time.

That guidance may come from a friend or other human guide: a spiritual teacher, a loved one, a professional counselor, or even a stranger sitting next to us on the train. Other people are often the best choice in helping us find the wisdom we have within ourselves, but sometimes we can gain powerful insights from the nonhuman voices that live in this world alongside us—the trees and rocks, the ferns and rivers, the eagle, the honeybee, and the possum. If you include unseen beings in your personal path (such as angels, saints, ancestors, and nature spirits), they too can provide profound guidance in times of need. We move and live in a world that is not fully visible to the naked eye.

All of these sources can help us to tap into our inner wisdom—a wisdom that may be difficult to hear when we are caught up in the chaotic noise of daily life.

This begs the question: Is there something that can help us find our answers when we feel stuck? How do we learn to listen to these deeper messages?

Divination is a method of seeking guidance from the inner self with the help of these other sources. In this way, you could say that divination is a type of language or conduit for communication, whether this is with spirits outside of yourself or with your own intuition. Divination can also help access your deeper, intuitive unconscious so that you can see new potentials and possible outcomes of specific choices or paths and find possibilities that the thinking/judging mind cannot perceive.

There are two types of divination that we'll discuss in this chapter. The first type enlists a set of tools that create stories or patterns for the seeker to interpret; the second involves a well-known shamanic approach wherein the seeker asks the living world for guidance and then looks for messages in visions, dreams, or signs. Both types of divination can be used, sometimes even in the same ceremony, to seek guidance in many situations.

There are a couple of things to keep in mind for both approaches. First, the questions you ask are just as important as the answers you will receive. Before you look for messages from your inner self or the living world, spend some time in deep contemplation with regard to your issue. How can you best present the situation so that you receive the answers you need to move forward? Sometimes yes/no questions are useful here, such as when you are using a pendulum, but in many instances questions that invite more depth will have a more profound impact on your inner work as a whole.

For example, instead of asking whether you will be offered a specific job you've applied for, consider seeking information on how you might use your gifts in ways that are meaningful and bring financial abundance. Open-ended, process-oriented "how" questions, combined with divination tools, can lead to a profound creative shift that opens up entirely new avenues. Divination approached in this way can also assist you in examining your old agreements and working to adopt new agreements that are more aligned to your soul's true purpose.

Second, it is important to remember when performing any kind of divination ritual or practice that life is a beautiful and wild thing, unpredictable and strange. Nothing is set in stone, and all messages received in divination should be understood the same way you might understand the advice of a friend. That is, they can lead you in a given direction or help you make a decision for yourself, but they cannot make your decisions for you or determine your future. You are the artist of your life, imbued with the power of your intent and nagual energy. No omen or image printed on cardstock can change that.

Throughout history, human beings have looked for messages in the fall of cards, stones, sticks, and other natural or man-made objects. Many of these methods are practiced even today, and I have included a list of divination practices with brief explanations of how to do them at the end of this chapter for further exploration. However, to begin I would like to share with you a unique divination and healing practice from my own family's tradition.

The Egg Ceremony

My grandmother was well-known in the community for her egg ceremony, which was part divination and part healing. The egg has long been a powerful symbol of birth, renewal, wholeness, and possibility. Many creation stories across the globe tell of a great egg that hatches the universe itself.

People would come to my grandmother in need of healing or when they had a big decision to make or were feeling stuck in life—and in all cases my grandmother believed that the life force contained in the egg could absorb any fear or negativity they were feeling, enabling them to step out of the addiction to suffering and make the best decision for themselves going forward.

As a *curandera,* my grandmother was able to use the same process to heal, as the life force of an egg would soak up whatever internal story, thought, or belief might be limiting those in her care and help return them to a state of wellness. In order to do this, she would take an egg, charge it with her healing intent and the openness of her heart, and pass it along the person's whole body. She would recite a prayer that was deeply meaningful to her—and to be clear, it doesn't matter what words were spoken; she chose those that were important to her and activated the faith she had in herself to be a conduit of change to heal others. I mention this because sometimes people think it's specific words that make the magic, but in my family's tradition it's not the words themselves that are important—it's the feeling they create inside you. For my grandmother it was Toltec and Christian prayers, but every shaman is different. The key is that the words connect them to the energy of being alive.

As my grandmother spoke her prayer, she began working the egg all the way around, gently rubbing it into the skin like a massage over the whole body. When this was complete, she would get a glass of water, crack the egg, and let the yolk drop into the water.

By looking at the egg in the water, my grandmother could see what was bothering the person she was helping. It was as though she had taken an energetic X-ray. She could accurately describe what the person was going through, where they felt stuck, and if they were in need of physical, mental, emotional, or spiritual healing. She could prescribe herbs or medicine, begin healing with her energy, or provide the person with other instructions to heal, all based on the results of the egg ceremony.

While working with a healer like my grandmother can be beneficial, there are other ways you can bring the powerful energy of the egg to clear your mind and get in touch with the wisdom within you. One way is to access the element of air by working with the egg on the forehead.

Mind Cleansing and Divination Practice

My grandmother explained that in the cosmology of the body, the forehead is like a great sky, the place where eagles fly. This makes sense, as our mind is the seat of our imagination. Divination opens and activates the imagination, creating new paths through uncertainty and creative solutions to seemingly unsolvable problems. For this reason, my grandmother taught that your mental space needs to be clear—because if the sky is full of smoke, the eagle cannot see all the possibilities that are available to you.

To begin this ceremony, find a quiet place you can relax. If you have a personal altar and can be near it while you do this ceremony that is wonderful, but it's more important that you find a place where you can be undisturbed for fifteen to thirty minutes.

Once you've picked your spot, either lie down or sit comfortably and center yourself. When you feel relaxed, think deeply about the question or situation that has brought you to this ceremony. What do you need help with right now?

Next, take a raw egg in your hand, close your eyes, and gently rub the egg over your forehead. As you do so, imagine the egg drawing in any tightness, negativity, or fear and that it is both healing and clearing your mind. Focus on the sensation of the egg on your forehead—its cool and smooth surface. Also bring your attention to your breath: as you inhale, imagine bringing in clean, clear air; and as you exhale, imagine you are blowing away any smoke that has clouded your vision.

When you feel complete, put the egg down and stay in this relaxed position for the next few minutes, focusing on your breath in the present moment and reminding yourself that the energy of the egg is still working to heal you and uncloud your vision. You may find that some new idea regarding the situation you are struggling with pops into your mind during the ceremony or within a day or two.

Personal Divination Ceremony

Prepare and gather:

- A candle and matches

- A journal or notebook

- A divination tool of your choice (optional)

To begin, take a deep breath and center yourself in the present moment. Let any regrets from the past or anxieties about the future drift out of your present consciousness. Notice your body and how it feels—particularly your feet planted firmly on the ground, no matter if you are sitting in a chair or standing, as these are your roots that connect you to Mother Earth.

Light the candle with a match. The sound of the match striking is like a bell to the unseen world, and the lit candle is a signal to the seen and unseen that you are beginning the work. Imagine that the light of the candle shines as a beacon to helpful spirits and your inner wisdom, calling on both to be here with you in this space at this time.

After you light your candle, ask for guidance through a simple prayer:

Spirits of the Earth, I honor you.

Help me find the best course of action to take,

Guide me on the path to wholeness,

And help me always to be in service to others, and to Mother Earth.

It doesn't have to be elaborate or fancy; you are simply asking for help from someone you respect (a god/goddess, the universe, unseen spirits, the living world, your higher self). Once you have opened yourself and invited the wisdom of the world to help you in this way, spend some time in contemplation. Then return your attention to your breath and the present moment, and release yourself from any inclination to "think" about your situation. You are clearing your mind so an answer may appear.

If you feel moved to work with a divination tool, now is the time to shuffle and lay out your cards, throw your stones, gaze into your cup of water, or look at your egg and see what comes to you from the living world in whatever method you've chosen to communicate. If you prefer the direct method, stay in this meditative state and see if a sign or idea rises into your consciousness.

If you feel you've received an answer, spend some time with it. You may find it helpful to write out your received message and any thoughts you have about it in a journal or other notebook in a stream of consciousness style. Keep in mind that you don't need to make sense of the message yet or know how it applies—for now, it's more important to remain open to the communication. Fold the paper and place it in your medicine bag or on your personal altar. You can return to your notes later to look for patterns and connections or to give you strength or insight as you navigate the situation.

You may come to a place where you don't feel your question was answered. When this happens, I often tell my students that this means "not yet." In other words, the nagual energy is not ready to provide you with any further direction at the present moment. The good news is that you have presented your question, and you can take the lack of an answer as an invitation to trust that more will be revealed to you in due time. While this can seem frustrating at first, when the answer to your question does eventually come, you will often be able to see why it had to wait to be delivered to you.

To close this practice, thank your inner wisdom and any spirits you called upon for their ongoing guidance. Just as you might want to bring a gift to a friend who has spent time with you and offered counsel, you may want to leave an offering of thanks, such as leaving cornmeal at the base of a special tree or pouring a cup of water out onto the earth.

Divination Tools for Further Exploration

There are many methods and tools used for divination. These few merely give you a beginning idea of how a variety of items, whether specially made or found in nature or in your own home, can be used to seek the wisdom of the larger world and draw on the deep reservoir of your own intuitive truth.

Bibliomancy

Bibliomancy is way to seek answers using books. The method is very straightforward: simply center your thoughts, concentrate on the issue you would like to explore, and then open a book at random and read the first passage that your eyes land on. Depending on your preference, you may wish to use a book by a particular author or that has personal spiritual resonance, such as sacred scripture or a special book given to you by a loved one.

Oracle Cards

There are many oracle card decks available today, featuring a wide variety of artistic styles, including animal/nature and shamanic themes. While some decks come with their own recommendations for use, the most common way is to draw a card at random and see what message it has for you.

Pendulum

A pendulum can be used by anyone without any special training to get a quick yes/no/maybe answer. You can purchase a pendulum or make one simply by attaching a small weight to the end of a short string or chain. Prepare to work with your pendulum by cleansing it or charging it with earth energy by burying it overnight. Sitting at a table, take a few deep breaths and ask for guidance and support as in the basic ceremony above. Each time you use it, start by asking the pendulum to show you a "yes." As you hold the string, the pendulum will make some kind of movement. Then establish a "no" and a "maybe." You can further solidify these distinct responses by asking questions that have clear yes/no answers, such as, "Do I have a dog?" or "Is my birthday in August?" Once these responses are clear for you, you can move on to asking the pendulum other yes/no questions. Note: pendulums are not very helpful when you are in an unbalanced emotional or physical state.

The I Ching, Runes, and Ogham

These tools are similar, as they all involve throwing sticks or inscribed stones onto a surface. All involve patterns and interpretation. The I Ching consists of a book of interpretations entitled *The Book of Changes,* which contains the interpretations of hexagrams that can be obtained by throwing yarrow stalks and discerning their patterns. With runes or Ogham, an early form of Celtic writing, the letters themselves are inscribed on individual stones and then allowed to fall on a pattern drawn on the ground or onto a special painted cloth. (Alternatively, a number of stones can be selected randomly from a bag.) Each letter contains its own set of meanings, and the seeker is able to string these meanings together to discern insight that applies to the question at hand.

8

CEREMONIAL SOUNDS

Take a few minutes and concentrate on the sounds around you. What do you hear?

Maybe it's the creak of a ceiling fan, the hum of electricity, or the wind buffeting the outside walls. You may hear animal sounds, such as the gentle snore of a pet or mourning doves cooing in the oaks or human voices calling out. Hear these sounds as if they were your favorite music. Savor them. Listen to the sounds farther away: planes droning overhead, the flow of traffic, a far-off radio playing.

Of course, you may also hear actual music, one of our most precious human gifts.

You may already know how important music is in my own spiritual practice. I love listening to recorded music and live concerts, and I am also an avid guitar player. In my experience, music opens the heart and quiets the mind, even when nothing else can, and especially in times of emotional distress or sadness. Music expresses what otherwise may be too big for words. Anytime you listen to music, it's an invitation to come into the present moment, which is a portal to the infinite.

Musicians know that making music can also be a powerful spiritual experience. Writing a melody, or lyrics for a song or a chant, taps into our inner wisdom and creativity. Remember, creativity is your birthright; you don't have to write a chart-topper to make good music— you are creating for yourself. Open your heart and follow its rhythm, and you may just find that words will flow on their own. Creativity is an act of drinking water from the infinite, a way of communicating with the divine.

One of my favorite stories about the power of creating music is from ten-time Grammy Award winner Carlos Santana. In a 2007 interview, he explains that his love for music came largely from his father, who had an incredible ability to play the violin and communicate with birds in the trees while he did so. "He taught me how to, with the violin, talk to birds," Santana once said, adding that "he'd do certain things with the bow and the violin, and then these birds come over and start looking at Dad, moving their heads back and forth. Then they start whistling back what he was saying."

Stories such as these make my heart sing. Since the beginning of time, music has been with us. When you explore any ancient spirituality, you discover some element of sacred sound. For instance, the Vedic Hindu scriptures of India, which are the oldest religious texts still in existence, famously discuss the Om, the sacred sound that corresponds to the creative power of the universe. In 2010, astronomers at the University of Sheffield were able to record the vibrations from the sun's coronal loops—bright arcs that appear above the sun's surface. Many people who listened to a video playing these vibrations interpreted these sounds as a universal Om. Whether or not the sun actually produces the sound of Om is less important than the fact that sound, in the form of vibration, is everywhere, and when translated through a human being's creative mind, spiritual richness and powerful meaning are the result.

My grandmother often used to say, "Let's make a sound!" Her father was a musician and a shaman, and he taught my grandmother that the moment we make a sound, we are heard. He would also remind her that the opposite is true—if we never make a sound, how can anyone hear us? Even if our sound is small, like a drop of water falling into a lake, from this tiny point the vibration amplifies outward in all directions. If you never make that first sound, you won't be able to see the ripple of your expression move out into the world. I often remind people of this when they tell me they have trouble speaking their truth to others: even the smallest sound can have enormous impact.

Sacred sound—whether it's music, chanting, or the nourishing tones of the natural world—also supports and provides healing. Researchers have studied a host of health benefits associated with humming and singing. Let's explore a few ways you can incorporate this ancient and powerful resource into your medicine bag.

Chanting, Singing, and Mantras

The human voice has extraordinary range, moving from a whisper to a shout and through every hiss, song, wail, and growl in between. With or without language, it can invite or banish. A single voice can inspire a crowd of thousands or soothe a baby with a soft lullaby.

Given its remarkable power, it's no surprise that the human voice has been a critical
part of spiritual ceremony and religious ritual
since the dawn of humankind. This ceremonial tool is always available to you. Chanting
and singing fill your ceremonies with a rich,
multi-textured resonance; when you lift your
voice in ritual, you are amplifying your intent
and broadcasting it to the universe at a vibrational level.

When you were a child, perhaps a grown-
up admonished you to not be so loud or told
you that you can't sing, and at some point you
believed this and stopped singing or chanting
at all. You might now tell yourself a story about
your voice, such as "I can't/shouldn't sing," or
"I need to keep my voice low and small so I
don't bother people." It's time to take any
old, restrictive ideas like these and send them
on their way. The beauty and strength of the
human voice belong to everyone. You have a
voice, and that voice has power.

You can begin to use your voice in a ceremonial way by chanting. In addition to the Toltec tradition, there are countless traditions that employ chanting, reciting, or singing as part of their observance. Benedictine monks chant, Jewish cantors sing sacred songs in Hebrew in synagogues, and Muslims recite the ninety-nine names of Allah. There are Native American sacred songs, neo-pagan chants, Buddhist chants for meditation, and many, many more.

I have a friend who has assembled her own personal chant/song collection from a variety of traditions over the years; some of the songs have been on "the list" for a long time, and others come and go. She mostly chants this personal sacred song compilation at her home altar, but she has also brought them out into the world. She's chanted by the side of the road on long car trips in gratitude for safe travel, to the trees in aspen groves to thank them for their beauty, and even while simply sitting on her couch during difficult times in her life. No matter where we might be on our spiritual journey, our voices are with us.

In the Toltec tradition, we say that chanting in this way is a type of meditation—a way to enter a state that quiets the chatter of the mind and brings you into the present moment. The words are important only insofar as they take you to this state where you can be deeply engaged and connected.

Chanting Ritual

First, you want to choose a mantra or chant that resonates with you. No matter how powerful a chant may seem (or how life-changing someone else may have told you it is), if it doesn't move *you*, chanting will feel more like a chore than a celebration. It is perfectly acceptable to begin with a simple yet powerful Om. In addition to Om, try the short chant that follows if you feel drawn to it:

I am the artist of my life.

I am the love of my life.

The beating heart of Mother Earth is my heart.

This is a perfect moment, a perfect time.

And I am dreaming a perfect dream.

Once you have a chant in mind, find a comfortable place where you can feel free to vocalize as loudly as you need to without feeling uncomfortable or worrying about disturbing others. Light your favorite incense, if you're using it, and take a deep, calming breath. Many rituals start with the breath, and when it comes to chanting, its importance can't be overemphasized. Breath is the vehicle for the human voice, and I encourage you to draw on whatever breathing techniques work best for you.

Allow your breath to move deep into your belly, and feel your whole self expand, welcoming the nourishment of oxygen and energy. As you exhale, imagine you are releasing all tension, fear, nervousness, and anxiety. You may wish to vocalize as you exhale, releasing tension with a clearing "ah" sound.

You may need to take several deep breaths to center yourself. Don't rush this process. The more comfortable you are with your sacred breath, the more powerful your chanting will become.

When you are ready, begin your chant with another deep, cleansing inhale, but when you exhale, allow your chant to ride the wave of your breath out into the world. Don't worry about musical notes or melodies—let the tone set itself naturally. Keep your breathing steady; if you find yourself out of breath or you are breathing too fast, that's often a sign you need to slow down. There is nothing to strive for here; no one is judging a competition for Best Sacred Chanting. There is only you, your amazing voice, and the great living world listening with joy. Chanting is a way to step beyond the thinking mind and be in the present moment.

Keep chanting your phrase until you feel it is time to stop. If you can only chant a few times before you are ready to stop, that's just fine. The quality of your experience is more important than how many repetitions of your mantra you were able to chant or how many minutes you spent doing so, though sometimes you may find that more time has passed than you realized.

As you become more comfortable with chanting, you may find longer chants that you feel drawn to. Don't be afraid to experiment or try new chants to see if they resonate with you.

Writing Your Own Chants

Writing your own chants can be a powerful way to connect with your inner wisdom. You do not need to be a poet or a songwriter to write meaningful chants, and unless you feel called to share, nobody needs to hear your chants but you.

For this kind of writing, it is helpful to create a sacred space and set aside a special time. You may want to write your chants in front of your altar or find a comfortable place in nature. If you wish, burn some incense and let the scent of it center you in the present moment.

Spend some time in meditation to see what topic you wish to write about. Perhaps you want to focus on a feeling you'd like to embrace, an attribute you'd like to cultivate, or a relationship you'd like to release. You can also consider writing a chant to express your gratitude or one that bolsters any of the other tools in your medicine bag.

When you know what your intention is for a specific chant, make a list of words and images associated with that intention. Consider your five senses—what smells, sounds, tastes, sights, and tactile experiences arise for you? Take your time, but don't overthink the list—let your intuition lead. For example, imagine you want to write a chant to help you cultivate more freedom in your life. Your list of words and associations may look like this:

Freedom

+ Flying over mountains

+ Birds

+ Travel

+ Soaring

+ Dancing

+ Moving forward

+ Breaking chains

+ Coming out of a dark space into light

+ Freedom tastes like fresh summer strawberries.

- Freedom smells like the desert after it rains.

- Freedom feels like bare feet in the grass.

- Freedom sounds like friends laughing together.

Now, looking through the list, craft a series of short phrases that incorporate some of these images. If you are chanting to bring something into your life, you may want to include "I am" statements, which signal to the universe that you are ready to receive these gifts. To follow our example from above, this may look like the following:

I am a bird soaring high over the mountains.

I am breaking the chains that bind me.

I am dancing into a new life.

You can also put some of your "sense" phrases together in a simple four-part chant.

For example:

Summer fruit,

Desert rain,

Freshly mown grass,

Old friends laughing.

I am free!

As you can see, your chant does not have to rhyme or follow any kind of special meter, though if you enjoy the challenge of writing in rhyme and meter, definitely do so. Additionally, as we explored in the chanting exercise above, you do not need to compose a specific melody for your chant, but if you feel moved to do so, it is helpful to record your chants so you can revisit them later.

Feel free to play around with words, sounds, and images until it feels right.

Rhythm of the Earth:
Drums, Rattles, and Dance

In addition to your voice, there are thousands of musical instruments that you can use to add music to your practice. One of my favorites is the guitar, but by far the most popular in most shamanic traditions are the drum and rattle.

Drums and rattles are earthy, grounded tools that tap into the sacred rhythm of the body and the heartbeat of Mother Earth. In the Toltec tradition, we say that the world has a heartbeat, just like you do, and when you listen to the rhythm of your own heart, you are listening to the rhythm of all life. In this way, drumming can activate and harmonize your mind with your heart, bringing you to a state beyond the storytelling mind.

Drums and rattles quiet the mind even as they activate the body. As the mind settles down and the body feels the music, it's only natural that it will begin to move.

While shamanic dance and drum circles are well-known, there are many traditions that make the connection between spirituality and dance. For example, the Islamic poet and Sufi mystic Rumi had followers so renowned for their dancing that they were soon referred to as whirling dervishes. In fact, sacred dance, like music and chanting, exists in nearly every culture and offers a rich and dazzling array of extraordinary costumes and diverse movements—everything from intricately choreographed dances to wild, ecstatic gestures.

Just as with chanting, you do not need any special training to participate in sacred movement. If you want to experience the power of drumming and dancing with others, seek out a local drum circle—or if you can't find one, consider starting one of your own. Likewise, this is something you can certainly do by yourself.

There are a number of drums and rattles available. Some have been lovingly crafted by hand from natural animal skin; others are commercially produced with synthetic drumheads. The drum or rattle you choose to work with is up to you, just as with power objects and items for your altar. The drum you see most often in shamanic journeying ceremonies is called a frame drum. It has a playing surface that is wider than the depth of the drum so that it can be held in one hand and beat with the other. The African djembe drums, which you often see in drum circles, are also popular. These can be played seated or standing with the drum between the knees and both hands free for playing. Usually just the hands are used to play djembe drums and there is no stick or drumbeater. Drums can be painted or decorated to make them unique to you and to increase the bond between you and your drum, just as you would embellish sacred objects for your altar or medicine bag.

Rattles come in a variety of shapes and sizes and, like drums, can be made out of many different materials and decorated in many different ways according to varying traditions. Be sure to choose an instrument that has a sound that resonates with you.

Inner Journeying with a Drum

Here is a very simple inner journey you can take to acquaint yourself with your drum and explore shamanic journeying. As a reminder, this kind of sacred journey is undertaken in the imagination, in a deep meditative state, and it expands the capacity of our intuitive mind to gain insight, answer questions, and/or cultivate transformation. This journey can also be taken with a rattle or other rhythm maker, but I will use the term *drum* throughout this exercise for simplicity's sake.

Find a comfortable spot where you know you will not be disturbed. You can be standing or seated for this journey, but make sure you are comfortable and have a bit of room for some movement. Lying down is fine if you are being led through your journey by another person, but if you are drumming for yourself, this might be difficult. If you have the room to do so and find it helpful, you might like to burn some sacred incense to cleanse the space. (Since you will be drumming and journeying within and may not be wholly aware of your physical surroundings, it may be best not to light any candles unless you can be sure of your safety.)

Take a few deep, cleansing breaths, and ground yourself in the present moment. Let go of any regrets from the past or anxieties about the future. In this moment, there is only you, your drum, and the living world. If you have spirit guides or powers to whom you pray, invite them to join you for this experience and to let their wisdom and their love flow through you and through your drum.

Close your eyes and beat a steady rhythm at whatever tempo feels best. Your goal here is to let the drumming come from within you, from beyond the storytelling mind. Imagine as you drum that you are calling out to the beating heart of the planet and it is drumming back to you in kind.

When you have drummed a steady rhythm for a few minutes, let the drum take you where it wants you to go. You may start drumming faster or slower, or a particular cadence will emerge. Your body may not be able to keep still; drums call the body to dance, and you may find yourself starting to move or sway to the beat. You do not have to be still to journey within.

As you continue to drum, picture in your inner mind a great forest. Look at the trees and note what kind they are—your forest will look different than anybody else's. Are you surrounded by fir trees? Redwoods? Or perhaps it's a saguaro cactus forest. Is it daytime in the forest? If so, notice how the light filters down and dances over all you can see. If it is night, say hello to the stars. Notice that you are standing on a dirt path that winds its way deep into this forest—so far you cannot see the end of it. Begin to walk along the forest path, knowing that you are safe and loved. Perhaps an animal or spirit guide will come and visit you. If you see anything unusual or interesting, take note of it for the future, but don't become too distracted by anything you see here; you can always come back later.

After you have traveled the path for the perfect amount of time (whatever that is for you), notice on your right that in one particularly enormous tree there is a door, which is just the right size for you. When you are ready, reach out and open that door and step through, knowing that when you come out on the other side you will be standing in your sacred space—your temple in the inner world. When you've arrived, look around and see where you are. Are you still outdoors? You may find yourself in a cave (an ancient symbol for the birth canal of Mother Earth) or on the top of a majestic hill beneath the moonlight. Perhaps you've moved indoors to a temple reminiscent of those in ancient Egypt. The possibilities are endless, but no matter where you find yourself, you realize that this place has been lovingly recreated in the inner realm and is your sacred space here.

Spend some time noticing how you feel while you are here—any sensations in your body as well as emotional responses. Again, you can make a mental note to examine these feelings more closely later on. For now you are simply spending time in this new holy space that is all your own.

When you feel you are ready to return, you may want to change the tempo of your drumbeat. This "returning" rhythm signals to your spirit to begin making the journey back to the present moment in this world. Retrace your steps, moving back through the door in the forest, and as you make your way up the path, renew your awareness of your body in the present moment. Slowly bring your drumming to a close, take a few deep, steadying breaths, and open your eyes.

I recommend that you spend some time journaling your experience. This will help you integrate what you've seen and learned, as well as remember the events and emotions you experienced along the way.

9

ENERGY TOOLS TO CLEAR
PHYSICAL SPACE

A dear friend of mine once went to visit a house that was for sale. She brought her kids along to see it, and the moment she stepped inside she felt an overwhelming sense of heavy sadness. This feeling was immediately followed by a strong instinctive need to protect her children. Without realizing what she was doing, she took her children's hands in her own and walked straight through the house—she did not even look around at any of the other rooms, all beautifully staged by the real estate agent. Her legs brought her fast out the back door of the house and into the yard, where she stopped and promptly burst into tears. But she had no idea why. She had no personal memories associated with the house and had never even been there before, but the energy had completely overwhelmed her. She had intuitively sensed something beyond the grasp of her thinking mind. Needless to say, she let herself and her family out a side gate and never went back.

Have you ever felt this kind of unexplained burst of emotion when walking into a room for the first time? It does not have to be negative, of course. Some places bring out a smile and a sense of positivity, or you may spontaneously find yourself saying, "Wow, it feels really good to be here." This might be a place of worship, a home, a workplace, or a public garden or museum. These spaces seem to be a celebration in and of themselves, overflowing with joy and peace and primed with potential for connection and positivity. Sometimes an older historical place will feel "heavy," overpowered by its difficult history, and yet a different space from the same time period will carry a sense of hope. When these experiences occur—whether positive or negative—you are sensing and reacting to the energy that is associated with a particular place. There is no scientific explanation for this that I'm aware of, yet we have all had this experience in one form or another.

While we all prefer to walk into a room that radiates joy, comfort, and love, you may also know how it feels to be in a space that has stagnant, negative energy. At the deepest level, this negativity is not real, of course, because the nagual energy that exists in all things is always life-giving and positive. But just as joyful emotions can make a space radiant with residual peace, negative beliefs and past actions from other people (or yourself) can leave leftover vibrational energy in a particular space, and these residual energies can influence our emotional bodies in very real ways.

These intense responses to particular places are relatively rare, however. More often, we may find it difficult to sense the specific emotional residue in a space, because we've become numb to its familiar energy—this can happen especially over time in our familiar spaces like our home or office. In the same way that we hold on to unconscious agreements, we can also lose energetic awareness of our space and the objects we choose to keep within it. Our homes and workspaces have the potential to be a pure reflection of our intent to operate in total freedom and with love, but if we lose touch with the sacred potential of our space, then apathy can set in or objects begin to clutter our space and get in the way of this freedom.

The good news is that you can easily bring calm, joyful, inspirational energy to any space where you spend time. One way to do this is through performing any number of clearing ceremonies and rituals that bring your intention of love and peace into the physical space around you.

Whether or not you are conscious of it, clearing your physical surroundings in this way is like opening a clear channel of connection to the earth—to the divine mother that is our home. The structures that we create and the design elements that we use for self-expression in our spaces can reflect and strengthen our connection to the nagual energy in all things. For this reason, we will begin with a powerful prayer that can bring healing to our physical bodies and extend positive energy into the spaces we inhabit.

The Palm-to-Palm Earth and Sun Body Prayer

This is a physical prayer that you perform with your whole body. Body prayers can help us go beyond the verbal or mental conversations with the divine that we often associate with the word *prayer*. These verbal or mental prayers are valid forms of prayer, but my tradition recognizes several different ways to pray that all have unique benefits. By experiencing more physical kinds of prayer, for example, we can tap into the body's inherent energy and power.

This ritual of blessing can be used when you are moving into or out of a new home or office and want to clear any energy from past traumas that are associated with the place. It can also be used to bless, create, or dedicate space for a special purpose—such as in preparation for an important event or at the start of a new project or venture.

To begin, rub your palms together vigorously, creating friction, as you might do in the winter to warm them up after coming in from the cold. As you do this, take eight deep breaths. It won't be very long until you start to feel the heat between your palms.

Next, bend down (or get down on your hands and knees, if you prefer) and place your palms on the floor—or any place that you have chosen to fill with positive energy. Close your eyes, take a few more deep breaths, and feel your connection to the earth. Imagine your body as a part of Mother Earth. Now imagine that via your hands you are sending a message to Mother Earth—this message is purely emotional and may involve feelings of love, peace, gratitude, healing, and hope.

Continue to breathe deeply, sending your messages of love and gratitude to the earth, and as you do so, you may feel vibrations of energy coming up from the ground through your hands. Just as you send love into the earth below, you are receiving the supportive love from Mother Earth back into you. Remember that the earth is always there supporting you, as you walk, sit, or lie down. There has *never been a time in your life when the earth was not there for you.* That is one reason why the planet is called the divine mother, because she loves and supports you all the days of your life.

Now that you have connected to the earth with your body, bring your mind into the practice. With your palms to the earth, say aloud this simple prayer:

Thank you for always supporting me.

From this moment on, I am in service to you.

Being in service to you is being in service to myself,

and when I'm in service to myself I'm in service to others.

Take a few more deep breaths as you send and receive this blessing. When you are ready, move your hands away from the ground and bring them in front of you again with your palms facing each other about one inch apart but not touching. Keeping your palms in this position, make circular motions, as if you are rolling a ball between them. As you do so, you will very likely feel an energy, or a vibration, between your hands. You can look right through the space between your palms—there doesn't appear to be anything there, yet you can feel the energy between them. This is the energy of Mother Earth.

Now open your palms and hold them still, as if you are cupping water, and imagine that you are holding a ball of energy. The truth is, you are. This is the energy of Mother Earth, of the nagual that is inside us all. Imagine all the stars and planets circling around within this ball you are holding in your hands. The same energy in the most distant stars is the energy that is in you right now, because everything is connected.

Now stretch your arms straight out and turn your palms upward, facing the sky, and send that amazing Mother Earth energy out into the space around you. The energy you felt when your palms were only one inch apart is still there, and you can gently push and move it through the air with your hands—into the corners of rooms, through closets, along floorboards, or out into the trees and grass if you are outside. Your prayer has become a ceremony that bestows the blessings of goodness to all you see. You are creating an atmosphere of love and peace in this physical space, with the knowledge that you are a messenger from the divine, in service to Mother Earth.

Salt Cleansing Ceremony

In some cases, you may want to do a more in-depth energetic clearing of your space. Like the palm-to-palm prayer, this ceremony opens up the connection to our divine mother and brings her presence into our space. Of course, her energy is always there—there is nothing on Earth that is not infused with her presence—but this ceremony can open a door to a wider awareness of this energy, amplified by our intent to be of service to Mother Earth and to our homes and personal spaces. It's especially good to do this ceremony in the evening or at night, because the light from the candle can be the brightest source of light in the room.

Prepare and gather:

- Your favorite incense (optional)

- A few teaspoons of salt in a small ceremonial bowl made of ceramic, glass, or another heat-resistant material (no plastic or wood)

- Water

- A white votive candle

- Drums, rattles, bells, or singing bowls (optional)

Salt has been used for centuries for cleansing. In this ceremony, you are going to tap the power of this natural wonder to do a deep cleanse of any room's energy. As you prepare for this ceremony, you may wish to light some incense to focus your intent and further enrich the space.

Pour a small amount of water into your bowl of salt—just enough to make a thick paste—and spread it on the inside of your bowl, covering the entire surface. Next, place a white candle in the bowl and light it while saying a prayer for the divine mother to bless this space. The salt bowl becomes a conduit for any corrupt energy, pulling it back into the earth, where it will be transformed and repurposed, as all things are.

You can amplify this clearing energy by including a cleansing sound vibration. This can be done with a steady drumbeat, Tibetan bowls, other kinds of bells, or even by plucking a single string on a guitar or violin. These vibrations can open a gateway for corrupt energy to flow away, leaving a crystal clear and purified space in its place.

Letting Go of Things

Another way to change the energy of a space is to remove objects that no longer serve you. In the same way we want to release things from our inner medicine bag that no longer serve us (self-judgment, addiction to suffering), we can also release objects from our physical space. It's easy to become numb to *stuff,* whether it's piles of paper, leftover objects from past relationships, or gifts we don't want to keep but feel guilty giving away. The mind has a tendency to identify who we are with what we have, and while this is the furthest thing from the truth, any buried feelings of negativity that you have associated with your "stuff," while you may not be conscious of it, will certainly cloud your energy and dim your intent.

Remember, things only have the power that you give to them through your agreements. That is, nothing is intrinsically "valuable" or even "necessary." One of the easiest and most obvious examples of this is money. Imagine someone hands you a stack of one-hundred-dollar bills. For most people, this would elicit a certain set of feelings—maybe excitement, gratitude, or relief. However, that stack of bills is really nothing more than a pile of paper printed with special inks. We give money value only when we, as a culture, agree to do so—otherwise, it's just processed plants and chemicals.

The acquisition of stuff has become so important in our modern world that what and how much we own can convey a powerful sense of identity and status. We get confused, thinking that what we *have* is what we *are*, and this is an illusion. For example, I've seen people on vacation get very upset if their suitcase gets lost in transit. It can ruin their whole experience and create massive amounts of drama. I wonder, is their suitcase going on a trip, or are *they* going on a trip? Outside of some basic necessities, our actual needs are few.

So I invite you to cultivate awareness about what you have and to be conscious when choosing your space and the things in it, as doing so is an outward acknowledgment that you are the artist of your life. Your space and the objects you choose to keep add to the colors with which you paint the masterpiece of your life, but ultimately, you actually only *need* very little. Below is a simple practice designed to help reconnect you to the authentic joy of your space and what you have in it.

Release Physical Items

Gather a pile of similar items you might be ready to release (e.g., books, clothing, kitchen utensils). Take a few deep breaths, and focus on the present moment. When you're ready, pick up each item one at a time, and pause while you listen to the voice inside you. Does it say "yes" or "no"? Only keep the things that elicit a happy or satisfied "yes." Go with your intuition, and try not to make your decision based on whether you "need" it or feel like you should like or keep it. Only listen to the yes or the no. For anything that is a no, decide quickly if it is trash or something you can give away or donate. While this exercise might be hard at first, it gets easier. Trust your gut and let go of those items that need to be released.

10

POWER JOURNEYS

Imagine for a moment that you are in a dream. In this dream, you find yourself walking down the street of a ghost town. You look around the alien landscape and feel lost, with no idea how you got there. But then something catches your eye. The faded business name printed on a building is the same as the company you work for. You then begin to make out the remnants of a few familiar things—a junked car spurs some memories, as does the smell of dust swirling around.

Suddenly, you realize that this ghost town symbolizes a particular area of your life—your job, a relationship, or some other life situation—and that like the ghost town you inexplicably find yourself in, the accomplishments or life situations that you'd been told would make you happy or into a "successful" person all feel like dead ends. You become absolutely certain that *something* needs to change, and you intuitively know that you don't belong where you are—but you're unsure how to move forward and leave this dusty, empty place behind and find a new, vibrant spot to call home.

As you walk farther, looking for signs that may lead you out of the ghost town, you are struck by a series of images: mighty rivers edging their banks, mountains nestled in thick clouds, an expanse of ocean that never ends, sacred stone ruins. Something is calling to you, telling you that you can't live here anymore, and you realize that you also can't stay in the situation this place represents. You realize it's time to wake up and change your Personal Dream.

If this story resonates with you, then you have been issued a powerful invitation. What actions can you take that will help you gain clarity and participate consciously in your own Personal Dream? How can you move forward into a more alive and dynamic landscape? One way is to embark on a power journey, where you can seek answers to questions and learn new lessons along the way, all as you work to make lasting changes to your Personal Dream and live the life of a true spiritual artist.

A power journey is a reminder that when we set our hearts and minds on making a change and combine that with action, we can transform the story of our lives. The power journey can take many forms: yours may involve a long pilgrimage to a well-known shrine, or it may be a shorter trip to an unknown but equally important spiritual place or engaging in a walking meditation such as a labyrinth. These journeys can even be internal, via meditation, visualization, or active imagination techniques.

The purpose of any power journey is to bring clarity and focus to whatever area you are struggling with and to travel from one state of being to another, letting go of old agreements that are no longer serving you in the process.

In this way, a power journey is not a vacation or even a spiritual retreat. While vacations and spiritual retreats have important roles to play in our lives, a power journey holds an altogether different meaning. A true power journey arises from an intense awareness that something in your life is ready for real, radical change. Many people describe this as a profound sense of clarity about a current situation in their lives, coupled with deep, difficult questions about what to do next. This is a call to the power journey.

So how do you use the journey as a tool in your medicine bag? This chapter offers three ways you can start. The first is by undertaking an actual journey—one with a geographical destination that holds sacred meaning and energy.

After that, we will explore the transformative power of walking a labyrinth, which can often be done relatively close to home. And finally, we will explore the inner power journey taken through the capacity of active imagination, meditation, and visualization. Just remember that in the Toltec tradition, *you* are the creator of your own story—so while you may find it helpful to travel a road journeyed by others, the gifts you find there will be for you and you alone. Even if you go to a place that other people hold to be sacred, you can only find the gifts of journey medicine in the places you know to be sacred *for you*.

Traveling to Sacred Sites

A wise auntie in my family always says, "There are certain things you cannot learn at home; you have to go away." There is practical truth to this and deeper spiritual truth as well. When you go through your days doing all the things you normally do, going to the same places and seeing the same people, you work yourself into a particular groove. Your routine prevents you from seeing things with fresh eyes, from opening to unknown possibilities, and from letting go of habits of mind and body.

In fact, it can be quite difficult to discern whether you are acting from your authentic desires or from the habitual ways you have been conditioned to act. But when you step outside of the familiar scenery and routines of your daily life, it can be easier to see yourself with the kind of clarity required to make real changes. The idea of a journey, then—whether or not it's a pilgrimage to a sacred site—is an ancient and essential part of the human story; it allows you to increase awareness of yourself while simultaneously drawing strength from a place of natural power. When you do so, you allow love to shine through you, and this love tells the true story of who you are.

A number of things can happen when you travel outside your familiar world—things that can have a lasting and profound impact on your life:

- You may leave the safety and security of your established community, which offers the chance to find a new community or expand the one you already have with the fellow travelers you meet along the way.

- You may find yourself alone, gaining the special wisdom that only comes from spending time in sacred solitude.

- You may face difficulties, roadblocks, and challenges, which offer the opportunity to learn how to overcome obstacles, adapt to new situations, and tap inner strengths you didn't realize you had.

- You may need to ask for, and gratefully receive, special help—whether from strangers you meet, the living world, or your inner guides.

- You may develop a whole new relationship to your home—through distance and perspective, you see more clearly the place you came from.

As I mentioned in the earlier chapter on power animals, observing a particular animal can inspire us in many different ways—and by appreciating their gifts, we are able to open a window into what is possible in our own lives. We see deer running free, and we commit ourselves to developing our own grace, agility, and the ability to be in tune with the world around us. We see a red-tailed hawk soaring above, and we are inspired to cultivate the gifts of keen perspective and pure freedom. In much the same way, we can be inspired by visiting sacred lands and places.

The Journey to Teotihuacán

In the Toltec tradition, there exists a sacred place that for many represents one of the tradition's most profound power journeys. This is the pyramid complex at Teotihuacán, Mexico. In the oral tradition of my family, it has been passed down that the Toltec people built this complex over twenty centuries ago, where it functioned as a thriving center for many on the path to personal freedom.

Today thousands of visitors each year marvel at the architectural accomplishment of the builders, but most don't realize that the plazas and pyramids at Teotihuacán together outline an incredibly powerful journey of spiritual transformation. My father, my brother, and I make regular trips there to lead groups on this journey. While the journey I describe next typically takes place over several days, I hope this brief overview can help you understand how a power journey may be used to cultivate personal growth and self-mastery.

The journey begins at the Plaza of Hell and the Temple of Quetzalcoatl, where seekers begin the process of looking at the agreements they have made in their lives up to that moment and discovering which ideas, beliefs, and assumptions they are holding that have turned their Personal Dream into a nightmare or their own version of hell.

The seekers then move forward into a period of intensive personal practices designed to bring about transformation as well as the reintegration of the spirit with the power of the divine feminine. Progressing through the plazas of water, earth, air, and fire, they then find rest and joy in the celebration of newness and rebirth atop the Pyramid of the Moon.

Finally, after a long climb to the top of the great Pyramid of the Sun (the third-largest pyramid in the world), the seekers experience the elevation of consciousness and the opening of ultimate personal freedom. Throughout the long journey they have faced the trials of their own hell, worked through layers of personal beliefs and agreements, and experienced a profound rebirth, all of which has served as deep medicine to transform their own consciousness. Now, they are ready to return to the world with a new perspective.

While Teotihuacán is an amazing place that is sacred to many, especially in the Toltec tradition, it is not the only place where one might experience such a powerful inner journey. You may feel called to any number of ancient sacred sites or to find the inherent spiritual intensity present in majestic natural places such as the Amazon jungle, the Chihuahuan Desert of West Texas, the African savanna, the high Himalayas, or a wide expanse of the Arctic tundra.

I also want to be clear that traveling to an exotic destination is by no means a requirement to experience transformation. The key to taking a power journey is to get outside your comfort zone and into an unfamiliar, meaningful place. So while traveling to a distant locale definitely fits this description, a power journey could also be to a nearby lake or nature preserve or even an old wooden church in the countryside outside your hometown.

When we listen within, the journey will call to us. Why? Because the nagual is always within us, and by its very nature it seeks creative expression and expansion. The nagual invites us to use the power journey as a tool to activate transformation in our lives.

Creating Your Own Power Journey

Prepare and gather

- A spirit of surrender

- A willingness to step into the unknown

- Your chosen destination

- Paper and pen or other tools to make a road map

The first step in taking a power journey is to acknowledge your inner call and pinpoint the situation in your life you are being led to explore. This is the ghost town in which you find yourself at the present moment—some aspect of your life that has become unlivable, empty, or frightening. Once you know what this is, resist the urge to think of solutions to your problem—that is the work of the power journey. The answers will come to you, but you need to be willing to surrender control for a little while so that you can walk the path with an open heart.

As you surrender and reaffirm your intent, you may want to say the following (adapting to your purposes as you wish):

> *As I walk the empty streets of the ghost town of _____ (my situation), help me to surrender to the power of my journey. Give me strength to let go of what is no longer working and faith to begin a journey toward _____ (my intent).*

The next step in beginning a physical power journey is to discern the sacred place that is calling to you. You may want to spend some time at your altar in meditation or simply ask the living world for guidance. Be aware of any deep yearning or images that rise to the surface of your consciousness, especially those that have an elemental quality. Are you seeking the fluidity of water, the thin, clear air of high mountains, or the mysterious embrace of an old-growth forest?

Once you have selected your destination, make a commitment to going there. Keep in mind that sometimes our creative energies open up new doors, so it's important to stay flexible in this. You may think that you need to go to a very specific place, but then an unexpected path will open up to another power journey. Follow your heart in this, and stay open to the process.

Before you physically go, you might want to make a kind of road map for yourself. Since you will be stepping into the unknown in a certain sense, having a general idea of your progression can be helpful to guide you on your way. This can take the form of space or time parameters, as in the case of the spiritual progression through plazas and pyramids at Teotihuacán. This can be as simple as choosing three powerful words or symbols for your journey to serve as waypoints that inspire a beginning, a middle, and an end. At Teotihuacán, these might be understood as the following:

- *Beginning*: Rising from hell (visiting the Plaza of Hell)

- *Middle*: Journeying through the elements (visiting the fire, air, water, and earth plazas)

- *End*: Ascending consciousness (climbing the pyramid)

Your journey can be a progression through any combination of symbols, spirit animal guides, elements, or attributes. You might consider using some of the divination ceremonies from earlier in this book to guide the creation of your power journey road map. Whatever you settle on, the goal of the journey is to amplify your personal power through your direct actions mixed with the potency of a spiritual place. Wherever you choose to travel, it will serve as a living witness for the new intention you are bringing to your life, and by visiting this place and engaging with it in an embodied way, you are bringing the gifts and energies of the space into your heart and mind.

Write down your road map or place symbols of your planned journey on your altar or in your medicine bag.

When you are ready to go, remember that your journey will help you on the path to personal freedom. Everything that happens in life has happened—we cannot change the past. But we can change how we live with our past and what we make of our lives now based on our past experiences. Freedom is the realization that you are the artist of your life. While you can read about the process in books or listen to someone else talk about it, there is nothing quite like the journey—the physical, emotional, and spiritual experience—of realizing what you truly are. If you don't like the art you are creating, only you can change it.

One more note before you embark:

You are the love of your life.

Others will come and go, but you are the one who will be there from start to finish. Know that a power journey will bring you face-to-face with this most important, unique relationship and offer you the opportunity to encounter yourself as the divine love of your life. You get to meet yourself and ask, "How do you want to spend the rest of our time, my love?" Everyone at their core wants to stop the negativity and fear that keep them in a state of suffering. A power journey can help you give yourself permission to finally let go, be truly free, and embrace your relationship with yourself.

Walking the Labyrinth

The second way to participate in a more local version of a power journey is to perform a walking meditation with a labyrinth. Labyrinths are ancient designs that have been documented in many cultures. Just as totems are symbolic of certain powerful energies in the world, the labyrinth is both a symbol and a practice reflecting an internal spiritual journey. A labyrinth can be anything from a drawing on paper that you trace with your finger to a fully assembled pattern on the ground that you move through as a walking meditation.

For this exercise, you want to find an image to work with or do an online search to find a labyrinth near you. You may be surprised to learn that there are many labyrinths in churches and secular spaces around the world. As of this writing, the website *https://labyrinthlocator.com* is a good resource.

In a way, the labyrinth is built to intentionally confuse the thinking mind. The twists and turns are a means to silence the inner judge and critic and return you to the present moment and your physical body. This feeling of being "lost," but still safe within a process that is leading you onward—and inward—brings peace and deep reflection.

The traditional labyrinth is not a maze—it does not lead to any dead ends, only slowly and irrevocably to the center of the circle. This center is a powerful metaphor for the innermost self, where your deepest truth lies. It is difficult to live from this deep inner place at all times—you have to navigate the outside world with all its many obligations. That is why it is all the more important to take time to go on the short journey that brings you to center.

Once in the middle, there is time to do whatever brought you to this meditation. You may want to reaffirm an intent, let go of something heavy that is weighing you down, ask a question, or just open your heart with trust that the right path will appear before you.

Once you have spent time in the center of the labyrinth, you return to the world along the same path. But as with a longer power journey, you are changed and renewed.

Once you walk the labyrinth, you see how it can be powerful in a number of situations:

navigating grief, problem-solving, resolving conflict with others, exploring feelings of loneliness or getting overwhelmed. And you can return to this simple journey again and again. Each time you practice, the labyrinth offers new insights.

Practicing the Inner Power Journey

The third way to go on a power journey is via your imagination, meditation, and visualization. Below is a short exercise that will allow you to get a feel for what a journey like this may be like. You may choose to adapt this meditation or write one of your own, especially if there is a sacred place you have already visited that has great meaning for you and that you would like to visit again in the inner worlds.

To start, settle into your space and take a few deep, centering breaths. Light your favorite incense and let the scent calm you and clear your mind.

Imagine, as you did in the beginning of this chapter, that you are walking through the dusty streets of a ghost town. Take your time in this space and notice the color of the dirt beneath your feet, the shape and state of the buildings on either side of you. Do you see any plants or other life, or has this place been completely abandoned? You know already that this location is a symbol for something in your life that has reached its natural end and requires your attention. Is it a job, a relationship, a routine, or a stagnant point on your spiritual journey? What area of your life needs the transformative power of your intent to foster true change?

In addition, you notice that you feel heavier than usual as you walk through the town, and you realize this is because the pockets of your jacket are full of stones. No matter how you try to remove them, they never seem to lessen in number.

Now imagine that you have reached the edge of town and before you is a beautiful wilderness. Is it a forest? A desert? An ocean? No matter how it manifests, you know that this is a place of deep restoration and inspiration. Just seeing this space after walking so long through the dusty ghost town lifts your spirits. This is the way forward.

However, just before you step out beyond the edge of town and into that new world, you find that your path is blocked by one of your spirit animals. It tells you that in order to move forward into the world you see beyond the limits of town, you must let go of a belief or agreement that has been holding you back in regard to the life situation you have been thinking about. This may take some time, so don't feel that you must resolve this in a single journey session—you may need to come back and do some journaling and meditating before returning another day and proceeding.

If you already know what you need to release and you feel ready to do so, reach into your pocket and pull out one of the stones. Tell your spirit animal what you need to release, and fill the stone with your intent. The stone is now a symbol for the belief or agreement that has been preventing you from moving forward.

When you are ready, let the stone drop to the ground. Feel the weight of it lift from you and know that you are free. Thank your spirit animal for its help, and take your first steps into your new life. If your new world is a forest, imagine the feel of shade on your face after standing so long in the sun. If it is an ocean, let the waves crash over your feet. Feel in your heart that you have taken your first important step toward true freedom.

When you are ready, return to the present moment and take a few deep, cleansing breaths. You may wish to journal about your experiences. Drink a glass of water and give thanks again to your spirit animals.

This is just a first step, of course. From here you may wish to write your own journey, releasing more stones from your pockets and moving further into the new life you are creating.

▲▽▲▽▲▽▲

No matter which approach you choose—visiting a spiritually significant place, performing a walking meditation, or visualizing a new way of life—power journeying can be one of the most life-changing practices you'll ever encounter. Often, that willingness to be open to change—and uproot old agreements to make room for new ones—is just what's needed to spark the inner artist within.

CONCLUSION

It is time for the wolf to return . . .

When we set out to walk the path of the shaman, we embrace the great task of bringing the self into balance. Through the loving application of ritual and ceremony, the honoring of the natural world, the creation of sacred space, the cleansing of our hearts, the connection to Mother Earth, and the honoring of our ancestors, we are able to heal ourselves, and through this healing we begin to see the world with new eyes—the eyes of an artist fully awake to the Dream of the Planet and committed to changing our own Personal Dream for the better.

This is the path of transformation.

The tools, ceremonies, rituals, and exercises in this book are offered as starting points on your own unique path as the artist of your life and the dreamer of your own dream. By practicing them regularly, you will become even more adept at noting the places in your life in need of healing attention, which in turn will assist you on the path toward authentic freedom and spiritual awakening. If you feel called to do so, you may wish to seek out a community of others interested in ceremony and ritual; this can be a wonderful way to share your journey and learn from others.

Your work with your medicine bag serves this journey—both the physical bag that you may wear around your neck and your symbolic medicine bag filled with your beliefs, agreements, assumptions, and stories about yourself. By learning how each item in your medicine bag either enriches or diminishes your life, and by making changes to its contents through the rituals and ceremonies in this book, you participate in an awakening process that has life-changing potential.

This is a critical time for the creatures of this planet. By increasing our awareness, awakening to the dream, and becoming artists of our own lives, each of us becomes a part of the greater movement toward healing and love for all.

ABOUT THE AUTHOR

Don Jose Ruiz was born in Mexico City, Mexico and was raised in Tijuana, Mexico. From a very young age, Jose was guided by many teachers present in his life, including his mother Maria, his father don Miguel, and his grandmother Sarita.

As a Nagual (the Nahuatl word for shaman), Jose brings new insights to the ancient wisdom of his family, translating it into practical, everyday life concepts that promote transformation through truth, love, and common sense. Jose has dedicated his life to sharing this Toltec wisdom, and he travels the world helping others find their own personal truth.

In addition to *The Medicine Bag*, don Jose Ruiz is also the author of *The Wisdom of the Shamans* and the coauthor of *The Fifth Agreement*, which he wrote in collaboration with his father, don Miguel Ruiz, author of *The Four Agreements*.

Hierophant Publishing
8301 Broadway, Suite 219
San Antonio, TX 78209
888-800-4240

www.hierophantpublishing.com

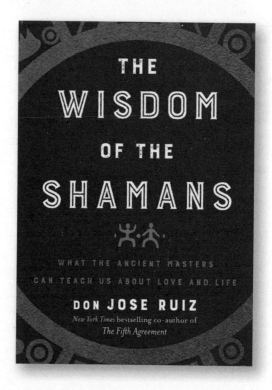